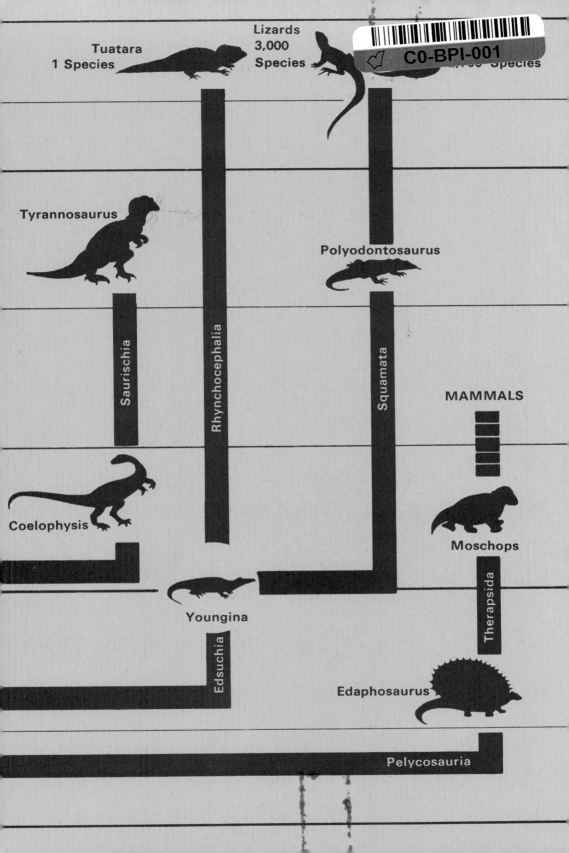

The Fascination of Reptiles

Maurice Richardson

The Fascination
of Reptiles

Illustrated by Shaun Milne

 **HILL** AND **WANG**   New York

A division of Farrar, Straus and Giroux

Copyright © 1972 by Maurice Richardson
All rights reserved

ISBN: 0-8090-4433-1
Library of Congress Catalog Card Number: 75-166468

First American edition 1972

Printed in Great Britain

Contents

List of Illustrations

Acknowledgement and Thanks

I should like to express my thanks to Margaret Lane for allowing me to quote freely from her *Life with Ionides* published by Hamish Hamilton; and to Desmond and Ramona Morris for allowing me to do the same from their *Men and Snakes* published by Hutchinson. I am also most grateful to James Stern for letting me make use of his short story 'The Man Who Was Loved' published in *The Stories of James Stern* by Secker and Warburg; and to Marion Jospson for providing me with herpetological reminiscences of her childhood in America. I would also like to express my thanks to the London Zoo for giving us facilities for drawing and photographing reptiles, and in particular to Mr David J. Bull, Overseer at the Reptile House, and Mr Lanworn, the Herpetologist.

Acknowledgements are also due to the following for permission to reprint poems and prose extracts:

For extracts from *Confessio Amantis* by John Gower translated by Terence Tiller, copyright © Terence Tiller 1963, to Penguin Books Ltd; for 'A Narrow Fellow' by Emily Dickinson from *The Complete Poems of Emily Dickinson* edited by Thomas H. Johnson to Little, Brown & Co.; for 'Snake', 'Baby Tortoise' and 'Lizard' from *The Complete Poems of D. H. Lawrence* reproduced by permission of Laurence Pollinger Ltd and the estate of the late Mrs Frieda Lawrence to William Heinemann Ltd, and from *The Complete Poems of D. H. Lawrence* ed. by Vivian de Sola Pinto and F. Warren Roberts, copyright © 1964, 1971 by Angelo Ravalgi and C. M. Weekley, all rights reserved, to the Viking Press; for 'To a Pet Cobra' by Roy Campbell from *Selected Poetry* to the Bodley Head and Henry Regnery Company; for 'The Plumet Basilisk' by Marianne Moore from *The Complete Poems of Marianne Moore* to Faber & Faber Ltd, and from *Collected Poems* by Marianne Moore, copyright © 1935 by Marianne Moore, renewed 1963 by Marianne Moore and T. S. Eliot, to the Macmillan Company; for 'The Snakes' from *Creatures Great and Small* by Colette to Secker & Warburg Ltd and Farrar, Straus & Giroux; for extracts from *Reptiles of the World* by R. L. Ditmars, copyright © 1910 and 1933, renewed 1938 by Raymond L. Ditmars and 1961 by Gladyce Ditmars and Beatrice D. Stanchfield, to the Macmillan Company; for extracts from *The Goncourt Journals* translated by Lewis Galantier; for 'Snake Phobia' by Alan Moorhead, from *Snake Phobia* to *The Sunday Times*, and from *It Won't Bite* to *The New Yorker*; for the extract from *Alone* by Norman Douglas to the author's literary estate and Chatto & Windus Ltd.

Introduction

The word fascinating comes from the Latin *fascinum*, meaning a spell. It is an appropriate word to use in connection with reptiles because it implies ambivalence. You cannot be indifferent to a creature that you think is putting a spell on you. You may be attracted or repelled, or both. The herpetologist who makes a scientific study of reptiles ought in theory to be free from such subjectivity; in practice, being human he almost certainly is not, not totally anyway. Myself a keen amateur herpetologist since a very early age, I have passed through various phases.

Lizards and crocodiles fascinated me from about five onwards; snakes got hold of me a year or so later. I longed to catch them and handle them and look at them and find out about their habits. A stuffed baby alligator on the nursery mantelpiece seemed alive. My interest, I can see clearly now, was rather more magical than scientific, just as magic preceded science in human history. They had for me peculiar properties that made them different from other animals.

My attitude towards lizards was never ambivalent. They were good and beautiful, living jewels. The Goncourts' phrase 'the lizard with his gentle friend-of-man eye' would have described some of my feelings about them, though not all. For when a splendid green Dalmatian lizard, so big I could hardly get my hand round his body, gave me a sharp nip as I picked him up from the greenhouse floor where he was snapping at flies, I was pleased, not afraid. I interpreted the bite as a sign of vitality and rejoiced that he was thriving, for when he had arrived the evening before in a cardboard box from the Army and Navy Stores he had been sluggish with cold. My grief two days later, when the gardener trod on his tail, too high up for him to grow a new one, was acute.

And yet, by a few primitive peoples, lizards are more dreaded than snakes. They share the reptilian mystique. Is this due to the general revulsion attached to what Nannies used to call creepy-crawlies? If so it is based on bad observation, for the gait of most lizards is dashing and jaunty, a spontaneous exhilarating movement.

By the time I was eight I was spending hour after hour of my easter and summer holidays hunting the common lizard on a south-facing bank on a heathery common near the Budleigh Salterton golf links, walking at a true herpetologist's pace of two steps a minute, praying under my breath: 'Please God send me a green one with a long tail,' or even murmuring: 'I know a bank where the lizards teem',[1] and sometimes reciting: "Snake was in his cabin and a thousand miles away . . ." My favourite book was the volume on reptiles in the Rev. J. G. Wood's *Natural History.* His style influenced my conversation. 'Have you ever,' I would ask my father's friends, 'been in close proximity to an adder?' I tattooed a snake on the back of my left hand in Indian ink.

At first I divided snakes into simply good and bad, nonpoisonous and poisonous. The poisonous ones were interesting but too sinister. I went on adder-bashing expeditions and did not outgrow the habit until I was fifteen or more, when I read W. H. Hudson in praise of the beautiful milky blue of adders' bellies. The first adder I bashed was stretched out on the lizard bank. It was just before my eighth birthday. I trembled all over with fear and excitement. I raised my stick high above my head and brought it down with such a whack that the adder's bruised body flew up into the air and fell at my feet.

All nonvenomous snakes I regarded as friends with whom I could establish an instant rapport. I loved the cool, dry, muscular feel of their bodies, their sinuosity and the flickering of their delicate forked tongues. The best snake of all was the king snake of North America, nonvenomous and immune to the venom of other snakes, and, which endowed him with extra *mana*, a cannibal. When I read in Ditmars' *Reptiles of the World* how a king snake in the New York Zoo had got into the cage next door and started eating a cobra I longed to possess one.

[1] Thirty years later in Palestine, near Nablus, I found a bank where big lizards teemed. Scaly snouts were poking out of every hole.

I have long since outgrown any irrational horror of venomous snakes and regret that it is not safe to handle them. The green mamba now seems to me one of the most beautiful of living creatures. The marvellously patterned skins of the rhinoceros viper and the gaboon viper are just as, if not more, characteristic of them than their huge fangs and venom glands. Yet there are many people, not noticeably neurotic, who do not even pause to distinguish between venomous and nonvenomous snakes. To them all snakes are almost equally abhorrent.

Make a list of the mythical qualities attributed to snakes throughout history and you will find that most, though not quite all of them, are fallacious. 'Snakes are cunning.' Untrue; though capable of wonderful feats of specialised adaptation their brains are much smaller in proportion to the size of their bodies than those of mammals. Solomon remarked (Proverbs xxx) that 'the way of a serpent on a rock' is 'too wonderful'. True enough; and some people may tell you that snakes can think with their bodies. Though it is not really possible to compare the intelligence of different classes of animal, and with all my respect for reptiles, there are moments when I feel that to feed a rat to a python is rather like giving Einstein to a cannibal village idiot for his breakfast. (The analogy is not correct because the python is perfect of his kind whereas the idiot is not so.) The 'Wisdom of the Serpent' is a legend that has deceived imaginative people from the authors of the Book of Genesis to Kipling.

'Snakes are cruel. And not only cruel, but they look cruel.' The attribution of human qualities to animals is a subjective fallacy anyway; but you could, in fact, make out a case for snakes being less cruel than some animals, for they are exceedingly swift in despatching their prey – except for some of the nonvenomous nonconstricting snakes like our English grass snake which swallows frogs alive. The allegation that they look cruel is absurd, of course, based on, if anything, the fact that their eyes are adapted for seeing at short distances and can give what may seem like a bold fixed stare. 'Snakes are savage and aggressive.' Also untrue. Most snakes are timid animals and glide away into cover as soon as they are disturbed. Some species of nonvenomous and venomous snakes may stand their ground. A few such as the bushmaster, the black mamba and, possibly in the breeding season, the king cobra may attack; but stories of their pursuing men are grossly exaggerated. So are many other serpentine properties: length, size of prey, speed.

It seems, then, that snakes have a peculiar aptitude for attracting human fantasy. Some of their strangeness they share with the other groups of reptiles. They are all members of a class that once dominated the earth. We shall form a brief nodding acquaintance with some of their ancestral relations later on. And between reptiles and the mammals who are descended from them there is a wide physiological gap. Reptiles are, to use that emotionally toned expression, cold-blooded. Tortoises and turtles are never feared and attract fantasy of a rather whimsical type. Lizards, we know, can be objects of superstition and dread but to a lesser extent than snakes. Crocodiles are feared, and often unnecessarily, but generally in a more or less rational non-paranoid way.

The unique feature of snakes is their limblessness. There is no doubt about their evolution from some four-legged, lizard-like ancestor, though precisely how this happened we do not know. It may have entailed two stages, a degeneration and then a regeneration, a recovery from 'decadent' burrowing to 'progressive' tree-climbing. If it did so, one might suggest that the prototypical serpent managed to shake off some of the Almighty's curse which, as Demond Morris implies, seems almost to have had some intuitive perception of the snake's evolution. Milton in *Paradise Lost* follows the Genesis myth with some variations of his own. His serpent has 'a head well stored with subtle wiles', but until the Devil enters into him he is:

> Not yet in horrid Shade or dismal Den
> Not nocent yet, but on the grassie Herbe
> Fearless unfeard he slept;

After this the Tempter takes over and the entire ophidian character has to be refurbished, ready for philosophical seduction. Another of Milton's embellishments is to add to Adam and Eve's punishment for the Fall:

> Th'inclement Seasons, Rain, Ice Hail and Snow.

From the evolutionary point of view one might interpret this as a glacial period of sudden onset, the effects of which on fauna and flora would be far-reaching. It cannot by any stretch of imagination be made to coincide with the evolution of snakes from their lizard-like ancestors, which took place many millions of years before our own mammalian ancestors had turned their scales into hair.

I must tear myself away from Genesis, though not without mentioning the interesting suggestion of Claire and W. M. S. Russell that, because the serpent was a sophisticated Egyptian symbol, he would seem evil to the pastoral Hebrews. A far worse misrepresentation of all reptiles was made, very much nearer our own day, by someone who should certainly have known better: Linnaeus, the Swedish eighteenth-century botanist who laid the foundations of biological nomenclature. Not only was he, as the late Dr Malcolm Smith pointed out, a washout as a herpetologist; he suffered from insensate prejudice. Lumping the amphibians in as well he denounced them all as: 'these foul and loathsome animals . . . distinguished by . . . doubtful lungs and a double penis . . .' They were, he went on, 'abhorrent because of their cold body, pale colour, cartilaginous filthy skin, fierce aspect, calculating eye, offensive smell, harsh voice, squalid habitation and terrible venom; and so their Creator has not exerted his powers to make many of them.'

Another reason, arising from limblessness, why snakes should attract myths is the hypnotic quality of their undulatory movement. The first – and not only the first – time you watch a snake coiling you tend to experience a slight suspension of consciousness. Here, perhaps, is the point at which to turn amateur psychoanalyst for a page and consider the interpretation of the snake as a phallic symbol. According to this theory the snake suggests a penis that is living an independent life of its own. (The fact that lizards and snakes have a double penis, or to be more correct, two hemipenes, is probably irrelevant because most people are quite unaware of it.) The symbolic penis is regarded as a source of potency, fertility and all the attributes of paternity, including wisdom. The attitude to the symbol is not simple. It is admired and envied, dreaded and detested. In fantasy it may be transferred from men to women, in which case it may be invested with sinister qualities, like Medusa with her hissing serpents for hair.

The danger of being bitten by venomous snakes is a real enough reason for dreading them and regarding them as symbolic of death. The Freudians, however, with remorseless tautology, point out that venom as a symbol can also be interpreted as the opposite of the life-giving semen:[1] something that cannot be gainsaid. There is a good deal of evidence in folklore to support the theory of the snake as a phallic symbol. As the Morrises point out in *Men and Snakes*, 'mediaeval artists and writers paid meticulous attention to the Devil's sexual organ. This was often visualised as being snake-like, sinuous and possibly forked like a snake's tongue, a remarkable piece of equipment which apparently permitted the devil an unusually wide range of sexual activity.'[2] There is another symbolic aspect of snakes on which the Freudians have remarked: that is their resemblance to the bowels, and even to their end-products, the excreta. The fanciful picture of the snake, especially one of the big constrictors, as a gigantic living intestine is not so far-fetched. As for the faecal aspect, I remember as a child peering into the lavatory pan and thinking how the coiled black turd in the water reminded me of an engraving of a water moccasin, half in and half out of some murky swamp water in one of the illustrations to the Rev J. G. Wood's *Natural History*. Not of any great significance, perhaps, but it may serve as an additional pointer towards the ambivalence of our attitudes.

The health-giving aspect of snakes, their suppleness, incomparable digestions, and habit of renewing their skins, was recognised by the Greeks and Romans. Entwined snakes are still the emblems of the medical profession. Asklepios – the Latin Aesculapius – the Greek god of medicine was said to manifest himself in serpent form and snakes were kept in his temple at Epidaurus. At Rome in 293 B.C. he made

[1] An interesting development is the modern use of snake venom in medicine, e.g. the venom of Russell's viper as a blood coagulant in haemophilia and water moccasins' venom in the treatment of rheumatoid arthritis.

[2] An Irish poet, the late Patrick Kavanagh, with whom I was discussing the symbology of reptiles, suggested (not altogether seriously) that in matriarchal Ireland, where there are no snakes and only one species of lizard (*Lacerta vivipara*, see p. 52), the lizard might symbolise the clitoris of Kathleen ni Houlihan.

one of his serpentine appearances and stopped an outbreak of plague. He seems to have been a Freudian precursor for patients slept in his temple and Aesculapius gave his diagnoses in dreams which were interpreted by the priests. A small sacrifice was the fee, considerably less than the present-day psychoanalyst's five guineas an hour. The cure of impotence and sterility was a speciality. The Aesculapian snake, a delightful arboreal brown colubrine, mentioned elsewhere in this book, was sacred to Aesculapius. Native to Greece, its eccentric appearances in other parts of Europe, France, Germany and Switzerland, are probably due to the Romans having introduced it at their baths and spas. But for a fuller treatment of mythological aspects I must refer the reader to that fascinating book, *Men and Snakes.*

Biologically, reptiles are so interesting that they need no trappings of fantasy. The variety of forms is astonishing. The smallest lizard is less than 2 inches long; the largest, the karbara goya, is 10 feet. Snakes range from a few inches to 33 feet. There are lizards that can fly, or at any rate glide, and a flying snake that can at least parachute; there are sea snakes that seldom if ever come ashore, and burrowing snakes that scarcely ever see the light of day. One species of crocodile swims for hundreds of miles in the Pacific. (Did, he, one wonders, ever take a snap at Moby Dick?) The tortoises have been leading their slow secluded castellated lives undisturbed, save by man, for century after century; but the turtles are mobile as submarines.

Reptilian colours, always in perfect taste, beggar description. As I write this I have just come back from the Reptile House at the Regent's Park Zoo where I saw an African spotted wood snake, turquoise with a pattern of black. The green of a green mamba is a delight; so is that of a long-nosed tree snake. The scaly texture blends exquisitely with colours. There is one South American tree snake with an emerald body and a blue head. All these are more beautiful than anything you, or the Onassises or the Burtons, can buy at Cartier's. Add the European eyed lizard and you have a fortune.

The age of giant reptiles finished (actually there were always many smaller forms) some one-hundred million years ago. But the living reptiles who are still with us are very numerous and wonderfully well adapted. They may yet outlive our own exasperating race, though at present their existence, like that of most wildlife, is increasingly threatened and they are in need of protection. I hope this book may do a little to help them get it. It is written for the general reader and assumes no previous knowledge of herpetology, but I have tried to make it as accurate as possible. Classification has not been shirked, nor Latin names which soon trip lightly off the tongue. There are brief accounts of evolution, anatomy and physiology as well as habits. I hope the selection of species described from all over the world is representative enough. There is a fair amount of anecdote and human interest, and the last chapter consists of a little anthology of reptilian *belles lettres*, verse and prose extracts, from Virgil and Ovid to D. H. Lawrence and Colette.

Chapter 1

Classification and Evolution

I have tried to simplify the classification as much as possible, though not, I hope, at the cost of accuracy; and I have restricted it to living reptiles, though the relationships with extinct forms are indicated.

The living members of the CLASS REPTILIA are divided into Orders as follows:

ORDER RHYNCHOCEPHALIA: this is limited to a single species, *Sphenodon punctatus*, the lizard-like living fossil (see p. 29).

ORDER CHELONIA: the tortoises and turtles.

ORDER CROCODILIA: the crocodiles, alligators and their very close relations, the gavials.

ORDER SQUAMATA, which is divided into two Suborders:

SUBORDER SAURIA: all the lizards, legged and legless.

SUBORDER SERPENTES: all the snakes.

The reason why the word sauria is used instead of some derivative of lacerta is because the latter has become restricted for scientific purposes to one family of lizards: the lacertidae. Zoological classifications often contain irritating features and though they are changed from time to time the changes are not always improvements. Unfortunately, for many people sauria and saurians mean the crocodilians.

It may surprise you to find lizards and snakes in the same Order, but the relations between them are surprisingly close.

Many, indeed most, of the Orders and Suborders are divided up into subsidiary groupings: families; sub-families; genera; and species. The grass snake, *Natrix natrix*, is a member of the species

Natrix, of the genus *Natrix*, of the subfamily *Colubrinae*, of the family *Colubridae*, of the Suborder *Serpentes*, of the Order *Squamata*, of the Class *Reptilia* . . .[1] In a popular book of this kind it is, I think, legitimate in many cases to dispense with the subdivision genus, and go straight from subfamily to species.

In the evolutionary scale reptiles rank between the amphibians (frogs, newts and salamanders) and the mammals. They are one of the largest and most important classes of the land vertebrates and we should respect them as ancestors. Mammals and birds are descended from reptiles. Mammals almost certainly evolved from them before the birds branched off. The duck-billed platypus (*Ornithorhincus paradoxus*) of Australia, that geologically ancient continent, is a link between reptiles and mammals. It is warm-blooded and hairy and in many other respects mammalian, but it lays eggs like a reptile and has typically reptilian shoulder-bones.

Reptiles, like amphibians and fishes, are described as cold-blooded; mammals and birds as warm-blooded. The popular terms cold- and warm-blooded are not properly descriptive. A reptile's body-temperature is regulated by the temperature of its surroundings, whereas a mammal can keep its body-temperature constant, irrespective of its surroundings. This vital difference is due to the fact that the rate of the metabolism of mammals is very much greater, about seven times, than that of reptiles. The best temperature for reptiles is comparatively limited, though it may vary somewhat with individual species. Heat above 100° F is as fatal as frost (many desert reptiles are nocturnal). The methods which reptiles may use for trying to regulate their body-temperature by moving from sun to shade, panting, and unrinating over themselves as some lizards do, are external; reptiles have no built-in method of temperature control such as mammals possess.

It is more difficult to warm up a large body than a small, and this

[1] The schoolboy, who is often innately scientific, likes to write his name and address on the fly-leaves of his textbook in fullest detail, beginning with the number and position of his desk, following with his postal address and ending up with: Planet, Earth; Galaxy, Milky Way; The Universe. His comment on our description so far would be that it is incomplete; he would insist on adding, correctly enough, that the Class *Reptilia* are members of the Phylum *Vertebrata*.

is why the big reptiles are only found in tropical regions. Most living reptiles are small animals. Only a few crocodilians are large. The longest snakes, the reticulated python of Indonesia and the South American anaconda, may reach a length of 30 feet and more, but the weight of even the biggest specimens is insignificant compared with the larger mammals.

The hardiest reptiles are the common viper and the common lizard which have been found north of the Arctic Circle. Vipers have even been seen basking on snow-covered ground; it is no accident that both are viviparous, the young being born alive though contained in a membrane while inside the mother's body. In general, despite individual variations, cold-bloodedness, or ectothermy, is a dominating factor in reptile physiology. Their slow metabolic rate makes it difficult for most reptiles to sustain long muscular efforts. They are creatures of fits and starts. Ectothermy apart, reptiles are closer to mammals than to amphibians and fishes. They are all air-breathing and do not go through any metamorphosis from a gill-breathing stage. Even the marine turtles, so well adapted to life in seawater, must come ashore to lay their eggs and are, of course, descended from a land ancestor.

Evolution often consists of forms turning into their opposites. Smooth-skinned amphibians living in water changed into horny-skinned, scaly reptiles living mainly on land. Later, the hard scales of some reptiles changed into the soft fur and feathers of mammals and birds. There is still discussion about which type of amphibian was the reptile ancestor, but it is thought that reptiles derived from one single amphibian stem. It proliferated into a wild variety of forms.

The earliest fossil remains of reptiles appear in carboniferous strata that date from the end of the Palaeozoic period about three hundred million years ago. The earth was covered with swampy forests of palm-like cycads and tropical conifers and ferns. There do not seem to have been any flowering plants or grasses, but insect life was rich. Some of the dragonflies had a wingspread of 2 feet.

There were probably three if not four main lines of reptile descent. One led to the dinosaurs (the word, literally, means terror-lizard), with a branch to the crocodilians. Another led to the ancestors of the lizards and snakes; another to the dynapids, which were to develop towards mammals. The origins of the chelonians are obscure. They retain some features that suggest affinity with amphibians, and others that suggest the opposite. Once they had developed their beautifully self-contained shells they could, as Bellairs puts it, 'relax and watch the world go by without having to undergo any more drastic changes'. A nice thought, though it rather begs the question of why some stayed on land and others reverted to water.

The proliferation of reptile forms took place mainly in the Mesozoic period. For a hundred million years the reptiles were the lords of the earth. Most spectacular were the dinosaurs. Some were no bigger than hares, but the largest were enormous. There were two main groups, one herbivorous, the other carnivorous. The herbivorous diplodocus measured 84 feet from snout to tail. The brontosaurus, with its preposterously small head on a long neck, was nearly as large. The carnivores that preyed on them and on the iguanodons – clumsy 15-foot-high creatures, with a hindlegged stance, that once roamed the Weald of England – were not quite so vast but large enough. A feature of their armament was their enormous teeth. The most formidable of them was the tyrannosaurus, 'the last word in reptilian frightfulness', as H. G. Wells called it. It moved on its hindlegs, specially adapted to take its great weight, while its forelimbs were too short to reach its mouth. Another large dinosaur, the herbivorous brachiosaurus which weighed about fifty tons, had well-developed forelimbs longer than its hindlegs. Aquatic reptiles included the plesiosaurus, around 50 feet long; the icthyosaurus; and one stupendous creature, the kronosaurus, which bequeathed to posterity a skull 99 feet long. There was the pterosaurus, or pterodactyl, of which Conan Doyle gave such a delightful description in *The Lost World* – though he probably exaggerated its powers of flight. These flying forms, with their large single-membrane wings, small limbs and relatively big bodies, were probably rather clumsy and vulnerable. Possibly more viable was archaeopteryx, the famous missing link between reptiles and birds, quite small, about the size of a raven, with avian feathers and reptilian teeth.

The Mesozoic period ended about one hundred million years ago. At this point there is a gap in the fossil record and when the trail can be resumed all the more sensational forms from the great age of reptiles are extinct. The suggestion of one single cataclysm that caught them napping is unlikely, though there certainly were global geological upheavals and changes of climate and plant life. Many species vanished with almost theatrical abruptness. Obviously, the giant forms were less fitted to adapt to sudden changes. It used to be thought that they were killed off quickly by cold; but a more recent theory, put forward by Bogert, suggests they were particularly susceptible to sudden rises in temperature and that they may have perished from heat! What about the many smaller forms? And how did the ancestors of the present living reptiles survive? Of these there remain some six thousand species – more than the number of species of mammals, though less than that of birds or fishes.

Of living reptiles, the chelonians and the crocodilians appear to have changed least. The evolution of the lizards and snakes is more problematical. There were some snake-like reptiles of great size during the Cretaceous and Tertiary ages, about halfway through the Mesozoic, and several smaller species like modern colubrines; venomous species do not seem to have existed before the end of the Mesozoic. The evolution of snakes from lizard-like ancestors has given rise to one speculation (you might call it the cataclysmic hypothesis) that all snakes are descended from small burrowing forms like the living sand boas. Burrowing habits may have had survival value during a period of cataclysm; later some of the burrowers may have regenerated. Changes in the size of an animal form during the course of evolution can be startling – e.g. the horse whose ancestry can be traced directly to the little five-toed eohippus of the Eocene period before the first Ice Age. But there is no certainty here.

One must be careful when thinking about animal evolution to avoid the tone of moral or value judgement implied in words like degeneration and regeneration. (I have heard an eccentric address a hen as: 'Wretched bird! You are so decadent. You have given up the power of flight!') Just how losing legs could have survival value is hard to imagine. Some of the surviving species of legless lizards, such as the slow-worm *Anguis fragilis* and the European glass-snake, have little of the true serpentine sinuosity and mobility; their movements, though gliding, are a bit stiff. They make, you may feel, an impression of arrested development. Yet no one who has studied slow-worms and watched them stalking slugs can deny that they are well adapted. Why one legless lizard should have stayed put while others evolved into snakes with their highly specialised movements is one of the many unsolved problems of evolution.

The snakes went on evolving during the Cainozoic age which followed the Mesozoic and spans the eighty or so million years between the end of the Mesozoic and today. In this they are unique among reptiles. One reason is that many snakes feed on small mammals and birds which, though they branched off from their respective reptile stems during the Mesozoic, did not proliferate until later.

Besides ectothermy there are other features common to all reptiles which must be mentioned before we turn to the different Orders and Suborders, families and species. Some of these – scales and air-breathing – have been noted. Another important division between reptiles and amphibians is that the eggs of reptiles have large amounts of yolk like those of birds, and the young, when hatched – or in vivi-parous species born – are fully developed, mobile and – in the case of venomous species – equipped with functioning fangs and glands. The reptile heart has two separate aortic trunks, but the ventricle is not fully divided by a partition and venous and arterial blood are always to some extent mixed. The red blood cells have nuclei like those of fish and amphibians. The brains of reptiles are smaller than those of mammals, and the brains of snakes smaller in proportion to body weight than those of lizards. In general the reptile brain is more like that of a bird than a mammal. The chelonian brain has resemblances to that of the amphibians. The spinal cord extends to the end of the tail and there are local centres that are to some extent autonomous. The popular idea that a snake 'thinks with its body' is not perhaps so wide of the mark.

Reptile intelligence has not been much studied scientifically and reports sometimes conflict. There seems little doubt that while many reptiles show elaborate patterns of instinctive behaviour they are not good learners. But then they are all most unsatisfactory as experimental animals in the laboratory. One example of their specialised adaptation is that strange organ in the roof of the mouth, Jacobson's organ, which connects with the olfactory centres of the brain. It sorts out molecular messages collected from the air by the sensitive forked tongue.

It is not possible in a book of this kind to give a detailed account of the anatomy and physiology of reptiles. For these the reader is referred to the Bibliography. Here are notes on some of the distinctive features of reptiles as compared with other vertebrates; most of them are also described in the sections dealing with individual families and species.

The scales of reptiles are made of horny tissue rich in the protein keratin. In lizards and snakes the skins are shed regularly, bit by bit by the lizards, in one piece like a glove by the snakes. The large plate-like scales or scutes often develop into crests and horns and protuberances. In the crocodilians they form a defensive armour. In the turtles and tortoises they fuse to form a shell.

In most reptiles the teeth are shed and replaced more or less continuously throughout the animal's life, the replacement often following an alternating pattern. The teeth of most species are conical in shape. Exceptions are the venomous snakes, especially the viperines with their highly specialised poison fangs, and the chelonians which have beaks instead of teeth.

There are various peculiarities in the bone development and skeletal structure. In most reptiles there are no secondary ossificatory centres as in mammals. The reptile skull, though containing more separate bones than the mammalian skull, remains more cartilaginous. In the lizards and snakes not only the lower jaw but also the upper is articulated with the skull. In the snakes complete disarticulation of the jaws takes place, allowing great feats of swallowing to be performed. The most striking skeletal modification among reptiles is to be seen in the snakes. These have evolved from a lizard-like ancestor, losing their limbs in the process. All the vertebrae in a snake's vertebral column have ribs. There are as many as 400 vertebrae in pythons and colubrids and about 200 or less in some of the vipers. The interlocking mechanisms between vertebrae make for great flexibility.

The reptile's brain with its small cortex is closer to the brain of birds than that of mammals. Most of it is taken up by the corpus striatum which, in terms of behaviour, is 'a seat of instinct rather than of learning'.

The eye is well developed except in some burrowing species. In nocturnal reptiles there is often a vertical pupil. The eyes of snakes are short-sighted.

An important sense organ is the organ of Jacobson, a modified part of the nasal sac. In lizards and snakes this has a separate opening into the mouth. It functions in cooperation with the forked tongue which brings it particles to sample.

Although the reptile ear is a complex system of tubes containing fluids and functions as an organ of balance, in many lizards and all snakes the middle ear has degenerated and there is no eardrum.

The reptile heart has two auricles and a ventricle often incompletely divided by a septum. As in the amphibians there is less separation of the venous from the arterial systems as compared with mammals. The red blood cells are oval and nucleated. Heartbeats vary considerably according to temperature. Heartbeat and respiration are much slower than in mammals.

In the snakes the lungs are much simpler than in other reptiles. There is either only one lung or only one lung that functions, with the other remaining vestigial. This arrangement, like other features of serpentine anatomy, is governed by the tubular shape of the body. The liver is much elongated; the kidneys are placed one on top of the other.

The mouth in reptiles extends behind the eyes; cheeks and lips are relatively fleshless. In lizards and snakes the tongue is highly specialised; in crocodilians and chelonians it is simple and immobile. The digestive tract is comparatively unspecialised. The cloaca is divided into chambers for excretion and reproduction; in some turtles it has an additional respiratory function. There are considerable variations in the physiology of digestion and excretion of ammonia and urea according to species and habitat.

The reproductive organs, testes or ovaries, are inside the abdominal cavity. The males of all living reptiles except *Sphenodon* have some form of penis. In most species of lizard and snake there are two hemipenes, one on each side of the cloacal vent. The oviducts of the females open into the cloaca.

An important aspect of reptile physiology is temperature-regulation. Reptiles are ectothermic, or cold-blooded. Unlike mammals they have no means of maintaining the body temperature at a steady rate. Their metabolism is slow and generates little heat. For warmth they are almost entirely dependent on the sun and their immediate surroundings. They are also very susceptible to heat and have no cooling apparatus like the sweat glands of mammals. They regulate their body temperature by behaviour, by sunning or shading themselves or by adjusting the angle their body makes with the sun; also in some species, and to a lesser extent, by changes in skin colour.

Chapter 2

The Living Ancestor

No reptile deserves a chapter to itself more than the unique *Sphenodon punctatus*. This lizard-like creature inhabits a few tiny islands off the coast of New Zealand; one of these, Stephen Island, is a mile long; others near the Cook Strait between the North Island and the South Island are not much more than big rocks. *Sphenodon* has no living relations and belongs to an Order of which all the other members have been extinct for many millions of years. It is an object of veneration among herpetologists: a living fossil. It is now strictly protected by the New Zealand Government.

Sphenodon grows to a length of 24–30 inches. Its body colour is greenish-brown and there are little yellow spots on its scales. It has a crest of spines along its back and tail. The Maoris call it *tuatara*, which means spiky. At first glimpse it looks like a cross between an iguana and an agamid. It is clumsy and slow-moving but can snap quite efficiently at crickets and beetles and crunch up seabirds' eggs. It is always found in close association with seabirds, but though it eats their eggs, and sometimes their young, its favourite food is the cricket. It has large dark brown eyes and comes out from its burrow at night to hunt. Gadow, who kept half-a-dozen specimens for several years, remarked on its imposingly noble appearance, but found it a rather dull, uncompanionable creature; it has none of that jaunty vitality, that dash and verve, which distinguishes so many lizards. When handled it makes a noise like a frog's croak with an undertone of grunt. It lays eggs which take fourteen months to hatch, far longer than is usual in reptiles.

The sluggish *Sphenodon* has a low body-temperature, sometimes as low as 43° F. Its metabolic rate is lower than that of other living reptiles and some amphibians. It breathes about once in seven

Tuatara *(Sphenodon punctatus)*

seconds when on the move, and when inert it may not breathe more than once in an hour. Its survival in New Zealand is due to its adaptability to a temperate climate where there are no mammalian predators – apart from those recently introduced by man. A quietist mystic would be tempted to philosophise on Taoist lines about *Sphenodon*, inactive and unassuming, living on and on while all its more sensational relatives have perished.

In 1831 the skull of a *Sphenodon* was received at the British Museum in London and described as a hitherto unknown species of lizard. In 1867 Albert Günther examined a number of complete specimens and decided that *Sphenodon* was not a lizard at all but a close relation of fossil reptiles which had lived 170 million and more years ago during the Mesozoic period, the great age of great reptiles. He classified it in a separate Order of its own, the *Rhyncho-cephalia* (beak-headed).

There are several features that mark *Sphenodon* off anatomically from the lizards. One of them is an additional bone at the side of the head; this fixes the quadrate bone in place. Also the ribs of *Sphenodon* to which the muscles are attached. Perhaps the most remarkable difference of all is that the male *Sphenodon* has no penis – unlike the lizards and snakes, each of which has two hemipenes. In *Sphenodon* copulation has to be done by direct cloacal contact.

Another interesting feature is the third (or median or parietal) eye on top of the head. This is not peculiar to *Sphenodon*. It is found in varying degrees of development in several species of lizards, among them *Anguis fragilis*, the slow-worm. In the young of *Sphenodon* it is covered by a translucent scale which later thickens and becomes opaque. Compared with the main eyes it is very crude and vestigial, but it has a rudimentary lens and retina and ought, theoretically anyway, to be sensitive to light. Is it a relic of a once perfect eye? Unlikely. Or is it the survival of one of a pair of eyes which grew on the top of the head of some ancestral vertebrate that might have been akin to the lamprey? The pineal body, gland or complex, from which the third eye develops, is found in all vertebrates, including man, where it was believed by early anatomists and also the philosopher Descartes to be the seat of the soul. One school of thought maintains that in *Sphenodon* the third eye develops from the left part of the pineal body whereas in lizards it develops from the right part. The fact has not yet been established. Experiments with *Sphenodon* and those lizards in which the third eye is most marked suggest that it may function as a transmitter of sensations caused by the sun's rays, but there is no certainty.

Chapter 3

The Lizards

Suborder *Sauria*

There are about 3000 species of lizard, including the legless ones. They are if anything richer than the snakes in diversity of form, ranging from the huge monitors, of which *Varanus komodoensis*, the komodo dragon, is the king, to the smallest living reptile, the Caribbean dwarf gecko. *Sphaerodactylus elegans*; from the incomparable and fantastic chamaeleon to the most humdrum of the skinks.

Family *Iguanidae*. This is a large family of about 700 species almost entirely confined to the New World. The variations within it

Rhinoceros iguana *(Cyclora cornuta)*

are very great. The iguanas themselves include arboreal, terrestrial and marine species. Many are brightly coloured and have decorative appendages such as crests, spines and throat fans. Their tails are strong and can be used as weapons. Their tongues are broader and less deeply forked than those of other lizards, some of them being barely notched. Most of them are oviparous. Size may range from the 7-foot common iguana of South America to the tiny Texas tree uta, 4 or 5 inches long. Their distribution is from southern Canada to southern Argentina and the Caribbean islands. Outside the New World they are found only in Madagascar, that home of interesting wildlife, and – one species only – in the Fiji Islands. The similarity between the iguanids and the agamid lizards of the Old World is, as Schmidt and Inger remark, an example of convergence of species.

The average size of the iguanas is probably less than most people suppose, between 8 inches and 15 inches, because they are accustomed to seeing large specimens of the common iguana (*Iguana iguana*) in zoos. This handsome green dragon-like arboreal lizard with its fringe of dorsal scales and hanging dewlap and big round brown eyes with a dark pupil is many people's favourite. The mouth gives the impression of being turned down slightly in a wistful cynical smile, like that of the late Somerset Maugham in one of his mellower moods. The tail is long in proportion to the body. It is partly vegetarian like many of the larger iguanids and eats bananas, but needs a varied diet. (See Chapter 15 on captivity.) Most of the iguanids eat insects and small invertebrates. The big iguanas are themselves eaten by men. Their flesh is highly esteemed by Mexicans and South Americans, and in village markets you can see them still alive, cruelly trussed with wire. There was an absurdly sensationalised account of cooking an iguana in one of the novels of James M. Cain.

Another fine iguana is the Cuban ground iguana (*Cyclura macleayi*),[1] which is light mauve with a yellowish-orange belly.

In some parts of South America, where the country is open and grassy or rocky, the ground forms abound. One genus, the *Hoplocercus*, sometimes known as the weapon-tail, digs short tunnels. In the dry uplands south of Brazil the commonest iguanids are the

[1] The *Cyclurae* are among the most primitive members of the family.

smooth-throated members of the genus *Liolaemus*, of which there are more than thirty different species.

One of the most interesting iguanids is the marine iguana of the Galapagos Islands (*Amblyrhynchus cristatus*). This dark powerful lizard was described by Darwin in *The Voyage of the Beagle*. Other lizards occasionally swim in the sea, but the marine iguana is the only one that is really at home in it. It feeds almost exclusively on seaweed and dives down to gnaw it off the rocks. It sometimes grows to a length of 4 feet or a little more. On the rocks inshore it clusters together in groups. Schmidt and Inger counted seventy-five in a space 30 feet square on Narborough Island, some of them piled three deep. One could see how closely they crowd together, and how expertly they swim in the Pacific swell, in Peter Scott's recent television film. The land-dwelling species on the Galapagos is *conolophus*, a few inches shorter and rather stockier; it eats cactus plants, spines and all.

An interesting and beautiful subfamily are the anolids, which includes the delightful *Anolis* genus of southern North America and the Caribbean islands. These enchanting little 7-inch tree lizards are bright green with pinkish throats which they puff out like balloons. Typical species are the knight anole (*Anolis equestris*) and the green anole (*Anolis carolinensis*). In the breeding season the males engage in quite fierce fights. They square up to each other broadside on with throats swelling up and the skin of the neck erect, making them look larger than life. If neither of them gives way at this threatening stage, they go on to bite and shake each other vigorously until one, sometimes both, falls from the branch. Then they may climb back into the ring and go at it again, sometimes for an hour. A curiosity of *A. carolinensis*, observed by Dr George W. D. Hamlett of the Louisiana State University School of Medicine, is its mating habits. It mates from spring throughout the summer and the female lays the eggs singly at the rate of one every fortnight. Because of its ability to change colour, perhaps also because its eyes are somewhat deepset, *A. carolinensis* and *A. equestris* are often most misleadingly described as American chamaeleons.

The courting etiquette of the anolids, which is much the same for the rest of the iguanid family, is subtly different from the martial approach. The male puffs himself up but does not raise the nape of the neck nor bob up and down so menacingly. If the female is unwilling to mate and runs away she is not pursued far. The females of some species, notably the fence lizard and the collared lizard, may show revulsion by arching their backs rather like cats and hopping down on stiff legs. The male then realises his suit is rejected.

If the female is willing she may turn her head from side to side in a gesture which, say Schmidt and Inger, 'can only be described as coy'. The male, seeing his advances are accepted, comes close, to the side and slightly to the rear; he grips the female's neck with his jaws, clasps the top of her hindleg with the toes of his foot, slips his tail under hers and inserts one of his hemipenes. Mating lasts from three to ten minutes. The female is passive as soon as the male has gripped her neck.

I cannot possibly describe all the species, but there are several other interesting members of the family that must be mentioned.

For instance the crested lizard (*Dipsosaurus dorsalis*) is found in Nevada and north-western Mexico. It eats the flowers of the creosote plant, also insects and carrion. Sixteen inches in length, it is very fast on its feet and may run on its hindlegs only, like the basilisk. It is a desert-living lizard and can stand the highest temperature, 115° F, of any North American desert reptile. Its body cavity has a black lining which may help to protect it from ultra-violet radiation.

The chuckwallah (*Sauromalus obsesus*) is another desert dweller found in southern Utah, southern Nevada and north-western Mexico. It eats flowers, and is fat and slow. When it takes refuge in crevices it fills its lungs and swells out its body, making it very difficult to extract. Unfortunately the local Indians are fond of its meat and deflate it by puncturing it with sharp sticks.

Another fast-moving desert lizard found in north-western Mexico is the gridiron-tailed lizard (*Callisaurus draconoides*) which has been timed to do 15 mph.

Even more ingeniously adapted, perhaps, is the fringe-toed lizard (*Uma notata*). Its snout is wedge-shaped with the lower jaw countersunk. The nostrils have valves to shut out sand; the eyelids are thick; and the toes are fringed to form what Clifford H. Pope calls sandshoes. When escaping *Uma* dives into the loose sand and quite literally swims in it, holding the front legs against the body and paddling with its 'sandshoes' while making swimming movements with its tail.

There are also the collared and the leopard lizards generally grouped together in the genus *Crotaphytus*, though sometimes the leopard lizard is classed in the genus *Gambelia*. Both are large active lizards, inhabiting the south-western quarter of the United States, eating insects and small lizards. The leopard lizard (*C. wislizeni*), 16 inches, is the longer by 2 inches and slimmer. The collared lizard often runs on its hindlegs.

The earless lizards of the genus *Holbrookia*, inhabiting the western United States, are small 6-inchers preferring dry soil, eating insects and spiders. They give an impression, like so many lizards, of great inquisitiveness.

The genus *Uta* comprising some twenty species, found in the western United States and north-western Mexico, shows many small individual variations. Most are climbers. The largest is the Californian collared uta (*U. mearnsi*), 11 inches long. The smallest is the little Texas tree uta.

The fence lizard, sometimes called the swift lizard (*Scleporus undulatus*), is a typical member of its genus, often known as 'the spiny lizards', very common in dry parts of North America and Mexico and further south. The fence lizard lays up to seventeen eggs and sometimes digs quite a deep hole in which to bury them. Some species of *Scleporus*, however, are viviparous.

The weirdest genus of iguanid is *Phrynosoma*, comprising the horned lizards or horned toads as many Americans stubbornly persist in calling them. There are fifteen species and the degree of horniness varies from zero in the case of *P. ditmarsi*, named after Raymond L. Ditmars, to almost total – a head covered with large spines. These lizards are very small, $4\frac{1}{2}$ inches maximum, but they are aggressive and will bite when approached, though their bite is only a harmless nip. They also have an extraordinary habit of squirting blood from their eyes up to a distance of 7 feet. They range from extreme south-western Canada to Guatemala.

I have left until last my own favourite iguanids which are the genus *Basiliscus* of South America. The Brazilian banded basilisk (*B. vittatus*) is very fine; but truly magnificent is the double-crested

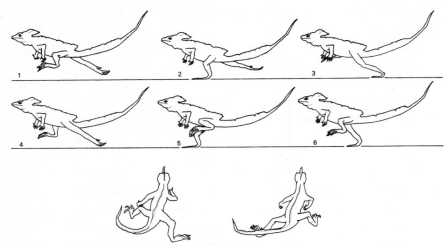

A   Gait of a basilisk lizard. Only two legs, tail used as a counter-weight to maintain balance

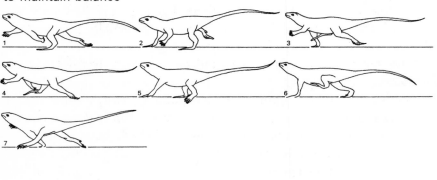

B   Gait of lizard running on four legs

basilisk (*B. plumbifrons*). Its head has a splendid streamlined crest like a flying angel's helmet, and the fringes on its back and tail are more unified than those of the common iguana which do, it must be admitted, look faintly tatty, suggesting the costume of a demon king in a provincial pantomime. The basilisk is partly arboreal; it can run very fast and may do 18 mph. It often runs on its hindlegs, is very fond of water and can dash for a surprising distance across the surface before it starts to swim. It too is partly vegetarian. Why should it have been given a name with sinister associations? Part of the reptile neurosis. I don't know whether the Brazilians dread the basilisk. I do know that the Portuguese, among the most superstitious people in Europe, tend to be terrified of lizards. I once distressed a Portuguese lady by asking if there were any lizards in her garden? She fainted dead away, collapsing under her own luncheon table. Her husband told me gravely that it was far better never to mention the word lizard at all, but if one must one should repeat it thrice: '*Lagarto, lagarto, lagarto*', as a charm.

Now for the agamids, family *Agamidae*. They resemble the iguanids closely in many ways but their dentition[1] is different and so is the arrangement of some of their scales. It is thought that while there are no agamids in the New World there may have been iguanids in Africa who were pushed out by the agamids except for those who took refuge in Madagascar. There are some 300 species of agamid, and they show if anything more variation than the iguanids. There are desert-dwelling, arboreal and aquatic agamids, and some remarkably – even eccentrically – specialised forms. The commonest and most typical member of the family is *Agama agama*, found in the Middle East and Egypt and other parts of North Africa. It is darkish, black to brown, about 1 foot long with a rather big head. It will peer at you from the top of a rock, bobbing its head up and down as if it were doing press-ups, looking comically menacing. When you approach it, it is off in a flash. Some Moslems are said to persecute it, or try to, because they say that it is blasphemously mocking their attitude when praying. A more eccentric-looking relation is *Uromastix*, a desert-dwelling species found in North Africa. This has a spiny tail and could easily be mistaken for an iguanid.

Some agamids vary their diet of insects and so on with a little fruit, flowers and leaves, but *Uromastix* is a total vegetarian and its teeth are modified so that in the adult lizard the front teeth drop out and are replaced by a sharp-edged growth of the upper jaw; the two

[1] The agamids have teeth on the crests of their jawbones, whereas the iguanids have their teeth set on the inner sides of their jawbones.

lower front teeth fuse together, giving the lizard a rodent-like apparatus ideal for biting off vegetation.

Strangest of all agamids is the flying dragon (*Draco maculatus*), a small arboreal species found in the forests of Indonesia and the Philippines. Draco is 8 inches long, green with bars of olive. Its fore-ribs are extended to support a wing-like flap of skin on either side of the body. This flap is black with bright orange spots. Draco cannot really fly like a bird because it cannot flap its membranous 'wings', but it can glide for distances of 40 feet or more.

The agamids, like the iguanids, are a worthy family – if I may be allowed a lapse into anthropomorphism. Despite all their variations they never tend to degenerate like the skinks. There are several superb agamids in Australia. The most sensational of them is the

Agama *(Agama bibroni)*

frilled lizard (*Chlamydosaurus kingi*), a large brightly coloured 3-footer which has an attachment of skin all round its neck. This can be erected to appear strikingly like an Elizabethan ruff. Indeed a frilled lizard with its ruff spread and its jaws open in rage or defiance strongly suggests Gloriana herself rebuking a courtier. What purpose the frill serves is obscure. Presumably, like the helmet-crests of the

Frilled lizard *(Chlamydosaurus kingi)*

basilisks, it may act as a frightener and deter predators. The frilled lizard is also a master of the bipedal gait and can run very fast on its hindlegs.

Another fine species is *Hydrosaurus amboinensis*, the water dragon, which looks like a cross between an iguana and a basilisk, and has a long tail flattened at the end and with a splendid crest along the base. It is greenish-bluish-greyish with lighter stripes.

Of the desert-dwelling agamids the oddest is *Moloch horridus*, a small Australian species that is covered all over with spines. This is the agamid homologue of *Phrynosoma*, the American horned lizard.

The incomparable chamaeleons are given a family of their own, the *Chamaeleonidae*, though they are thought to be of agamid ancestry. Their specialisation is very elaborate. I am giving them a chapter to themselves.

Now for the geckoes. Family *Geckonidae*. These have several anatomical features that distinguish them from other lizards. Their bodies are flattened. Their scales are small and granular. Their skin

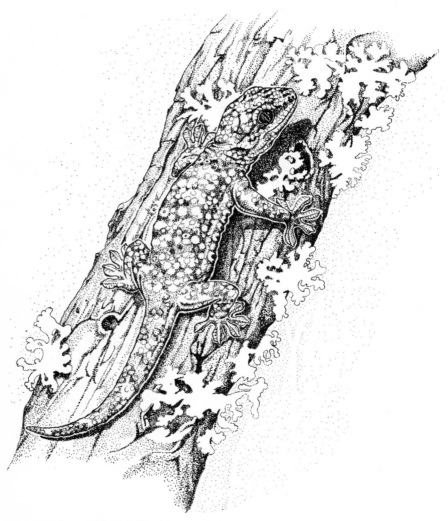

Malayan house lizard *(Gekko gecko)*

is so thin that some of them appear translucent.[1] In most species the eyes are protected by a spectacle scale (cf colubrid snakes) instead of eyelids as in other lizards.

There are numerous species, none large, some very small, barely 2 inches long. There are ground-dwellers and desert-dwellers, and in towns in the tropics geckoes have established themselves as house-lizards – perhaps the only example of a domesticated reptile. Most geckoes are insectivorous and nocturnal, and have specialised eyes with vertical contractile pupils. Also highly specialised are their feet. These are elaborately padded with plate-like ridged skin that can catch on to any irregularity of the smoothest surface, even glass. They do not, as most people suppose, work by suction. One African species even has a clinging pad on its tail.

Geckoes are distributed throughout Asia and Africa. They are found in the southern United States and South America, and islands of the South Pacific and New Zealand. Whether they are native any-where outside Asia and Africa is uncertain. They may have been imported or have travelled as stowaways under the bark of logs. Many species are grey or brown, but some are quite brightly marked and there is one species in Madagascar (*Phelsuma laticauda*) which has a bright green head, a red spotted body and a light green tail. It is diurnal, which may account for its fancy dress.

All geckoes are oviparous, laying tough leathery eggs with a long incubation period. Their mating habits are much like those of the other lizards and courtship includes tail-waving by the male and a certain amount of nosing and nibbling. They give one the impression of being sociable little lizards. This is partly because of the noise they make. Most reptiles are fairly silent. Snakes hiss and the crotalines rattle their rattle-tails. Crocodilians emit a kind of barking bellow to establish territorial rights and express desire in the mating season. Geckoes, alone, are vocal in a way that can be compared to birds.

Most typically vocal is the Malayan house lizard (*Gekko gecko*). This is the species, maximum length 9 inches, that used to be so familiar to Empire-builders and their wives. Many is the intimate scene,

[1] One tiny gecko which inhabited the ceiling of the sitting room of friends of mine who lived on the outskirts of Jerusalem was like a little ghost – thoroughly capable of taking care of himself, though.

whether of adultery, hysterics or even of rare connubial bliss, which *Gekko gecko* must have witnessed from its voyeur's lookout on the bungalow ceiling. The noises made by geckoes are variously interpreted. 'Gecko' is taken from the call of a common North African species. 'Cheechak', 'tuk-tu' and 'tokay' are attempts at transcribing the cries of some of the Asian species. They seem, as they scamper surprisingly fast across the ceiling, to be chirping to each other like birds. And why shouldn't they be doing so? Animals are not machines and the gap between warm-bloodedness and cold-bloodedness need not be exaggerated. Incidentally, though not accidentally, the gecko's ear is the most highly developed of any lizard's ear, with a complex inner structure.

Gekko gecko is brighter in colour than some if its relations and has orange spots on its back. It can be very noisy. There was one family of geckoes that used to haunt the ceiling of the billiard room in the club at Kuala Lumpur; they were said to answer the click of the billiard balls. In Indonesian towns thieves sometimes used geckoes for stealing hats. The gecko is lowered on a string from an upper window onto a passer-by's hat. Its pads and claws take a tight hold on the hat the moment they touch it. Fortunately the Malays are sensible about geckoes and think them lucky, but in some parts of Africa they are feared and persecuted.

There is one interesting Oriental species, *Ptychozoon*, which, with some stretch of imagination, can be called the flying gecko. It has a wide flap of skin, webbed toes and a flattened tail. Dropping from a height of 20 feet it parachutes lightly down. The smallest gecko is the Caribbean species, *Sphaerodactylus elegans*, which I have already mentioned. Its maximum length is 1½ inches. It has the distinction of being the smallest living reptile and, as herpetologists for generations have pointed out, it is shorter than its name. It lays only one egg at a time.

Now for the skinks. The large family *Skincidae* is widely distributed over most of the globe. Skinks have smooth scales, elongated bodies and, generally, short tails. All are small, none more than 2 feet long. There are some aberrant forms such as the rough-skinned stumpy Australian skink, but the family does not show anything like the variety of the agamids, the iguanids or the *Lacertilia*. They do, however, show a tendency to reduce their limbs, if not quite to the point of losing them altogether. There is, I think it can be said without undue anthropomorphism, something dull and 'degenerate' about skinks, though I would be happy to be corrected on this . . . they lack the brio and vivacity of so many lizards. Yet they are one of the most numerous families with over 600 species. You don't see them often because they lead unenterprising lives,[1] hiding under stones and vegetation. No doubt this secretive modesty is a reason for their abundance. And, for one must be fair, although they can hardly be regarded as examples of evolutionary brilliance they do show some quite interesting adaptations. There is one genus in Ceylon which has developed specially curved teeth useful for coping with its frugal diet of earthworms. The tongues of the insect-eating species, which are the majority, are thick and sticky, most suitable for making the best of an ant. Many skinks are burrowers and have strong conical snouts. The tails of many species are brittle and may be snapped off (as with so many lizards). This is a useful protective device to distract the predator while the skink escapes. A new tail is grown. Schmidt reports that a high proportion of the Great Plains skinks (*Eumeces obsoletus*) examined had had accidents to their tails. There are also cases of snakes which, on dissection, have been found to have nothing in their bellies but skinks' tails.

One type of behaviour shown by skinks that has less than no survival value is the fighting between males in the breeding season. In most lizard families this fighting is largely bluff, but the male skinks bite each other savagely.

There are several families of small legless burrowing lizards with reduced eyes that used to be grouped with the skinks but are now classed separately: the *Anelytropsidae*, *Feyliniidae* and *Dibamidae*. There are four species of *Feylinia* in Equatorial Africa, length about 1 foot. Their only defence seems to be feigning death.[2] They are dreaded by African natives who believe they can enter their bodies and cause death. Related are the *Xantusiidae*, a very small

[1] Perhaps the most exciting species is *Corucia zebrata*, the giant (22-inch) skink of the Solomon Islands which has a prehensile tail.

[2] A few snakes, as we shall see, have this trick. Nobody has yet discovered how it deters predators.

North American family, nocturnal, and faintly reminiscent of geckoes.

The *Anguidae* is the family that includes the slow-worm (*Anguis fragilis*) and the European glass-snake (*Ophisaurus*). These two are completely legless. The slow-worm is described separately in the chapter on British lizards. The glass-snake is very much larger – 30 inches plus, and lighter in colour. It is oviparous and the female guards her eggs. There are several related species in the Old and New Worlds. The eyes of most *Anguidae*, unlike those of the burrowing skinks, show no degeneration.

The *Amphisbaenidae*, so called because both ends look the same and they can move in both directions, are a small highly specialised group of burrowers with thick compact skulls. Their anatomical differences from other lizards are considerable and they are classed

Common tegu *(Tupinambis nigropunctatus)*

in an infra-order of their own. They are found in America and Africa and the southern parts of the Iberian Peninsula.

The family *Teiidae* is an exclusively New World family with a good deal of resemblance to the *Lacertidae*. Some species have what might be called faintly snake-like characteristics. The largest are the tegu (*Tupinambis nigropunctatus*), a handsome black and yellow lizard 3 feet long, and the 4-foot-long Caiman lizard (*Dracaena guinanesis*) of South America, which is aquatic. The teids are very varied and range from large active species like these to small lizards 3 inches long and some in which the legs have dwindled if not disappeared.

Now for the family *Lacertidae*, some 150 species. These typical lizards are confined to the Old World. There is considerable variation in size but few specialised adaptations such as we find in agamids and iguanids; neither are there any degenerations in the direction of limblessness as in the skinks. Lacertids have scaly bodies, pointed heads and well-developed limbs with long, clawed digits. The neck and body are covered with small, hexagonal keeled scales. The lower eyelid is freely movable. The outer ear opening is large and there is a well-developed eardrum. All *Lacertidae* are egg-layers with the single exception of the common lizard (*Lacerta vivipara*).

The *Lacertidae* are graceful lizards with well-proportioned bodies and long tails. The tails are covered with rings of scales; they are readily shed. The new tail is never so long or aesthetically proportioned as the original.

There are some desert-dwellers and two African species that have spiny scales round the base of the tail. Most lacertids are at home in any suitable dry habitat. They can climb easily enough and there are several species that live in forests, but the majority prefer dry bush country. They are essentially sun-lovers. There are a number of European species. One of these, the splendid eyed lizard (*Lacerta ocellata* or *Lepida*) of the Western Mediterranean with its beautifully marked body, speckled green with blue spots on the sides, is one of the largest, at 2 feet plus, and handsomest members of the entire family. Most lacertids are mainly insectivorous, but the eyed lizard eats other lizards, young snakes and even mice. It chases after its prey at speed with dash and determination, seizes it in its jaws and shakes it savagely, if necessary bashing it against the ground. When it has finished eating it licks its lips with its long, deeply forked tongue. One eyed lizard which I encountered on the cliffs between Port Vendres and Banyuls near the Spanish border stamped its foot at me three times before dashing away. *L. sicula*, found along the Dalmatian coast of Yugoslavia and in Greece, is distinctly larger than *L. viridis*, the beautiful European green lizard with its emerald back and delicate pale yellow belly. A giant form, *Lacerta goliath* which reached 3 feet 3 inches, has recently died out in the Canary Islands.

Colour variations among the lacertids range from green to brown with all kinds of variegated markings. Melanistic, jet black variations are quite common in some species, notably *L. vivipara* and also the wall lizard (*Lacerta muralis*) which is so abundant in southern France and Italy.

The lacertids are widely distributed throughout Africa. One species that deserves a special mention is the tiger lizard (*Nucras delalandi*). It has been seen adopting the following defence when attacked and about to be devoured by a sand snake. The lizard took one of its own hindlegs firmly in its jaws and held on tight, making a ring of its body. The snake, which was used to starting on lizards at the head, was frustrated. It began swallowing the tail but was baffled by the ring formation so it disgorged it and looked again for the head. The process was repeated several times. At this point Dr Rose, who reports the incident, intervened, restraining the snake with his stick; the lizard dashed away. One would like to think that this ingenious device, which set the snake an insoluble topological problem, would have succeeded.

Another interesting species which has adopted a rather unusual way of life is the Chinese grass lizard (*Takydromus septemtrionlais*). Clifford Pope describes this lizard making its way through high grass in the province of Anhwei by jumping nimbly from stem to stem, balancing itself by its long and very slender tail.

The common lizard and the sand lizard (*Lacerta agilis*) are described in some detail in the chapter on British lizards. In a general book like this I have no space to enumerate all the species of European, much less Asian and African lacertids. Lilford's lizard found in south-western Spain, and the little species native to the island of Capri, are examples. Some say there is a unique species on the island of Formontera off Ibiza. And some sceptical and possibly envious herpetologists grunt and say: 'Hm, a separate species to every island . . .'

The family *Varanidae*, the monitor lizards, contains one genus in which there are twenty-one species distributed over Africa, Asia and Australia. And what magnificent species they are. Among them is the giant komodo dragon or karbara goya (*Varanus komodoensis*), which grows to 10 feet long plus and weighs 300 lbs. The smallest monitor is a short-tailed Western Australian species, *Varanus brevicauda*, 8 inches long. All are oviparous.

The monitors – goannas, they call them in Australia – are all unmistakably similar and characteristic in appearance whatever their size. They have long heads, long necks, long bodies, long claws, and long tails which are not fragile but can be used as powerful weapons. They seem to be designed for mobility. They have neither crests nor spines; their pattern is strictly functional. The skin is loose and a little baggy, a comfortable fit for an athlete in training. The eyes are large and bright. A monitor has an expression of utmost alertness. It really is a noble lizard.

From an evolutionary point of view the monitors are reckoned to be one of the oldest living lizard families with an ancestry going back to the Mesozoic. They are thought to be related to a group of aquatic prehistoric lizards of the Cretaceous period, the *Platynota*, whose cousins, the *Mosasauridae*, produced giant sea-going lizards like Tylosaurus over 30 feet long. In some ways the monitors have a closer affinity with snakes than any other lizards. (The resemblance is most marked in *Lanthanotus borneensis*, the earless monitor of Borneo which is now classed in a family by itself. Its skull is remarkably like a python's. The tongue – as with all monitors – is very long for a lizard and deeply forked. There is no eardrum and Jacobson's organ is well developed.) There are no traces of the ancestral burrowing monitor which must be assumed to have been a suitable ancestor of the snakes, but that is no reason why it should not have existed.

The monitors live in desert, brush, scrub and forests. Some have flattened tails for swimming. They are splendid all-rounders and it is a little surprising that so well adapted and vigorous a family should not have become more dominant.

Two outstanding examples of the larger species are the Malayan monitor (*Varanus salvator*) and the Nile monitor (*Varanus niloticus*). Both these are almost equally terrestrial, arboreal and aquatic. The Malayan monitor is a huge lizard up to 6 feet long which digs burrows for itself in river banks. All monitors are voraciously carnivorous; anything goes down their gullets: fish, lizards, birds, mammals. They are particularly fond of eggs. An additional affinity with snakes is seen in their feeding habits. They are inclined to bolt their food and swallow it whole. The huge komodo dragon will even eat small deer and pigs.

Nile monitor *(Varanus niloticus)*

The large Australian lace monitor (*Varanus varius*) is heavily addicted to eggs and goes climbing after them. Yet it has been routed by cockatoos, who are fierce defenders of their nests and which attack the lizard's eyes.

A monitor's disposition varies with the temperature. In captivity it may seem quite tractable and even take food from the hand, but you cannot be sure that it won't lose its cool. At New York's Bronx Zoo a couple of komodo dragons which had just arrived and were recuperating from the voyage seemed docile as a schoolboy's pet lizard. It was a warm day, so their keeper put them in an enclosed yard to give them an airing in natural sunlight. After half-an-hour he looked in to see how they were getting on. They hissed loudly, hoarse rather wheezy hisses somewhat different from the shriller hiss of a snake, and the one which was nearest him manœuvred sideways and lashed out with its tail, inflicting a painful weal.

Alas, the size of monitors and the toughness of their skin make them subject to persecution by commercial lizard-hunters.

The family *Helodermatidae* consists of the two species of poisonous lizard: The gila monster (*Heloderma suspectum*) and the Mexican beaded lizard (*Heloderma horridum*). *Suspectum* inhabits Arizona, parts of Texas and New Mexico, and Mexico. *Horridum* seems restricted to Mexico. They are much alike and rather hideous in shape, lacking any of the lacertilian graces. They have large blunt heads, tiny beady eyes, thick bodies with warty-looking scales that don't overlap properly and bloated tails, useful for storing fat. Both are mainly black or very dark brown with salmon pink, sometimes whitish, markings. *Horridum*, with a maximum recorded length of 31 inches, is larger than *suspectum* at 22 inches. They were first described, and quite accurately, in 1577 by a Spanish colonist, Francisco Hernandez. Though desert-dwellers, they are fond of water and in captivity sit in it for hours.

The heloderms are sluggish creatures and either squat around waiting for their prey to come near or else choose prey that can't move fast such as fledgling birds and very young mammals. Their venomous apparatus is cruder than that of the snakes. The venom glands are connected with the lower jaw, not the upper; the 'fangs' are grooved. The venom has affinities with that of the elapid snakes (cobras, etc.) and is neurotoxic in action. It is moderately powerful; its effect on man can be quite severe, though deaths are very rare. Both *suspectum* and *horridum* are docile in captivity and let themselves be handled; some reptile-house keepers are said to develop quite an affection for them and swear they will never bite unless outrageously provoked. But when they do bite they hang on like bulldogs and it is the devil to make them let go. The tenacity of their grip and the smallness of their prey make one wonder whether their venomous equipment is really necessary[1] unless it is for defensive purposes. Their pedigree, I should mention, is respectably ancient. A fossil ancestor some forty million years old was discovered in Colorado.

[1] A Spanish friend with whom I was discussing this anomaly told me that all the eccentricities of animal evolution could be explained by the hypothesis that the Creator was not always strictly sober.

Chapter 4

British Lizards at Home

You can't expect reptiles which, with certain qualifications, are lovers of warmth and the sun, to flourish in the British climate. One of the most poignant sensations of the northern herpetologist when he first arrives in a southern country and finds a suitable habitat – rocks, scrub, bush or wall – is the entrancing profusion of lizards. Snakes, with some exceptions, are fonder of cover and generally need to be sought out. You can spend months in a tropical country, even India, without seeing a snake, but outside of towns, and sometimes inside them, there are moments when lizards seem to be everywhere, including the ceiling.

However, the British herpetologist with a proper scientific spirit, who can eschew sensationalism about size and colour, has six interesting species, three lizards and three snakes, to study. The lizards, to which I am confining myself in this chapter, are the common lizard – *Lacerta vivipara*; the sand lizard – *Lacerta agilis*; and the legless slow-worm, sometimes misnamed blindworm – *Anguis fragilis*.

Lacerta vivipara is a typical member of its family, the *Lacertidae*. It is a small lizard, maximum length $5\frac{1}{2}$–6 inches, with very varied coloration. This in Britain can range from several shades of brown to a slightly vague shade of green; there are generally broken black markings down the back. The underbellies of the males are dark orange with merging black spots, of the females a uniform light ochre. In one spot in Devonshire, a heathery common with a bank at the edge of a pinewood, which was a paradise for *L. vivipara*, I noticed local colour variations within a distance of a few feet. The greenish specimens I found, almost without exception, in little

Common lizard *(Lacerta vivipara)*

clumps of heather and grass just inside the wood. Melanistic or black variations are said to be quite common, but in many years of lizard-hunting I have only caught two, both females; the backs and sides were black as jet. I was nine years old when I caught the first of these and thought at first I had discovered a new species. A sympathetic postcard from the Reptile House at the London Zoo disillusioned me. My melanistic female had meanwhile escaped; this was my first lesson in the remarkable escapological expertise of so many reptiles.

The diet of *L. vivipara* consists of flies, spiders, other small insects and their larvae, and sometimes small earthworms. They drink water from the dew that collects in leaves. They are expert swimmers. If you put them in a tank they swim fast with a serpentine movement of the tail, their 'arms' and legs flat against their sides. Although they prefer a dry habitat – a heathery common with a southern aspect is ideal – you sometimes find them in marshy ground.

Near Lamorna in Cornwall I found one on a stone in the middle of a small pond; it must have swum to get there. You find them in hedgerows, on cliff tops, wherever there is heather or gorse, sometimes but less often on sand dunes and by the seashore. The specimen I found on the stone in Cornwall had a birfucation of the tail, which had two ends like a little forked stick. The tail of *vivipara* is a fascinating organ. Be very careful how you handle it, for it breaks easily. The severed end wriggles frenziedly for a minute or two and goes on twitching for some time. The ease with which the tail is shed, and the sensational behaviour of the severed end, which acts as a distraction to a predator, must have considerable survival value. The device might work if the predator were a bird, but I can't see it succeeding with the viper, which is one of *L. vivipara*'s main predators. A new tail is easily grown even when the severance takes place quite close to the hindlegs, but it is cartilaginous and has a clumsy makeshift look compared to the fine elegantly tapered original, and is always a good deal shorter. Most of the *Lacertidae* have this tail-shedding propensity, but it seems, perhaps because of the lizard's small proportions, to be particularly marked in *vivipara*. The tail always breaks neatly across a vertebra and the severed column is protected by spike-like protrusions of flesh. A tailless specimen seems little the worse for the injury and darts away in a flash.

The distribution of *vivipara* in the Old World is very wide. It is found all the way across Europe and Central Asia, all the way from Ireland to the island of Sakhalin. It is in fact the only reptile in Ireland. The reason for this is thought to be that *vivipara* was the first to reach Ireland after one of the later glacial periods and then became marooned there by whatever geological cataclysm it was that cut Ireland off from the main land mass. It is not very profuse there in spite of the absence of its chief predator, the viper. (The Irish have a legend that St Patrick lured the last viper, symbol of sin and evil, into a stone box and shipped him out of the country.)

The name *vivipara* comes from the lizard's method of reproduction. The young, generally from five to eight of them, are born alive, directly from the mother, inside whose body they are, as it were, hatched out. All other members of the genus are egg-laying. There is, however, one variation of *L. vivipara*, found in the Pyrenees, which lays eggs; why the Pyrenean females should retain the primitive method of reproduction is as yet one of those lesser unsolved biological mysteries.

Mating, after a limited amount of fighting between rival males, takes place in April and May. There is no preliminary courtship; the female may allow the same male to mate with her more than once, though she will snap at him when she thinks she has had enough. The period of gestation is about three months. The female deposits the young in some suitable sheltered cavity. They emerge in a thin membrane from which they thrust their way out. Within a few hours they are running about and able to feed themselves. A newly born *vivipara* is about a quarter of an inch long and dark bronze in colour. They stay bronze, though tending to get progressively lighter with the markings beginning to emerge, until they go into hibernation.

All species of lizard can be said, with perhaps a slight stretch of imagination, to have 'character'. (If you interpret the word as meaning a distinctive collection of characteristics it doesn't sound so anthropomorphic.) The character of *vivipara* is essentially dashing. This little creature is full of natural *élan*. All its movements are quick and darting. It dashes about in short sharp rushes as if moved by some inner spring, yet gracefully. With its delicate, almost spidery, clawed toes it is an expert climber and can dash up a perpendicular gatepost almost as fast as if it were on a flat surface. It shows no fear when caught, bites your fingers as hard as it can and hangs on like a little bulldog, though its teeth are so small that they seldom draw blood. Yet, within a minute or two of being caught, it becomes tame and allows you to handle it. It thrives in captivity so long as it is given proper food and a suitable roomy environment. The Belgian herpetologist Rollinat has kept *vivipara* for five years. Some specimens are particularly fond of brown sugar.

The sand lizard, *Lacerta agilis*, is rather larger and thicker than *vivipara*, also a great deal rarer with a very limited distribution. It grows to a length of 8 inches. In colour it is light brown or almost grey above, with dark spots with a whitish centre. The belly is cream with white spots. The males in the breeding season have bright green sides and their backs may occasionally take on an almost purplish tinge; they look beautiful, lizards to be proud of.

In Britain, where the sand lizard is unfortunately becoming increasingly rare, it is now only found in parts of Surrey, Hampshire and Dorset (which, significantly, are also the haunts of the now even rarer smooth snake, one of its predators), and, somewhat eccentrically, near Southport in Lancashire. It is a genuine sand-lover, likes burrowing, and often makes use of tunnels left by mice and voles. The adjective *agilis* is a misnomer. The sand lizard is inclined to be rather slow and deliberate in its movements. Its diet of insects and spiders is much the same as that of *Lacerta vivipara*, but it tends to be more of an omnivore and will go for butterflies, moths and beetles. It gives its prey a prolonged shake and devours it at leisure.

As compared with the dashing *vivipara*, the sand lizard, though this really is going rather far in the anthropomorphic direction, might seem to have a strain of melancholy in its disposition. It has great need of sun and this makes it difficult to keep in captivity. Captive sand lizards in England rarely survive the winter.

The Belgian herpetologist Rollinat, who made an intensive study of sand lizards under ideal conditions in his walled rock garden, insists that the sand lizard is the most intelligent reptile in Europe and shows a capacity to learn which is much above the average for lizard species. His description of how he trained his lizards to take cockroaches from his fingers and come to be fed when he banged on his cockroach trap makes fascinating reading. Fascinating, too, are the accounts by Kitzler and others of the sand lizard's sex life. Mating, in May and June, is more elaborate and less casual than with the *vivipara*. Rivalry between the males is fiercer, with often quite prolonged fighting. When the successful male has won his mate he first seizes her by the tail, then twists his body in a semicircle, bringing his cloaca into conjunction with hers. The same pair of sand lizards will mate together many times. The females accept the males without hesitation. Rollinat describes one female who deliberately chose a male for herself, crawled over to him, deserting the male who was nearest to her, and whose attention she had already been attracting by shaking her forefeet. It may not do from a strictly scientific standpoint to class this kind of activity as love play, but there does seem to be a genuine courtship.

The sand lizard, fully oviparous, lays her pale leathery little eggs –

from six to thirteen of them – in June and July. She scoops a shallow hole for them and covers them up. The young, who are equipped with a sharp egg-tooth, measure about an inch or more when they hatch out, and put on half an inch more before going into hibernation in the autumn.

The slow-worm, *Anguis fragilis*, is a member of the small but widely distributed family of legless lizards, the *Anguidae*. Relatives include the so-called glass-snake, *Ophisaurus*, of Europe and Asia, which is equally legless, though some of the *Anguidae* have kept either vestiges of limbs or traces of them, or even very small though quite well-formed, still-functioning, limbs as in the case of the West Indian *Celestus*.

In the anguid lizards the limb-girdles, which you don't find in the skeletons of snakes, are still present together with other lacertilian features. Lizards they remain and it would be incorrect, since all animal evolution, so far as can be observed, is a process that has halted, to think of them as lizards on the way to becoming snakes.

Anguis fragilis grows to a length of 18 inches and is found in most parts of England, though commoner in the south than in the north. Its colour varies from a brownish or creamy grey to copper to dark brown. There is often a black line down the back and sometimes a quite clearly defined Y-shaped mark on the head. The late Dr Malcolm Smith, a leading authority on British reptiles, claimed that it is easy to distinguish between a fully grown male and female at a glance. I've never found it at all easy myself. Even the belly colour, which should be uniform black in females, has misled me before now. I once dissected a slow-worm which I could have sworn was a male and found it was a pregnant female.

You can find *Anguis fragilis* in a variety of habitats, so long as they are dry. It is at home in hedgerows, banks, heaths, commons, gardens and churchyards. Sometimes, especially if it is a pregnant female, it will lie stretched out, sunning itself like a snake, but it is a secretive creature and likes to be near, or half in, cover. When disturbed it can move remarkably quickly, with a sudden gliding dive. If you grab at one and miss you probably won't get a second chance. It seems to have a trick of evaporation. It is helped in this by the extreme smoothness of its scales which, unlike those of most lizards, or snakes,

'Slow-worm' or 'Blindworm' *(Anguis fragilis)*

are almost invisible to the naked eye and give its body a uniform burnished appearance. The slow-worm is a natural burrower and if the soil is light it may go a foot or more underground; again it may lie in the earth with only its head showing.

Slow-worms will eat worms, spiders, insects and occasionally snails, but their favourite food is the small white slug. A slow-worm will stalk a slug with as much care and ceremony as a big-game hunter. It raises its head very deliberately for a matter of seconds, then seizes the slug by the middle, shakes it from side to side, and chews it slowly.

Mating takes place, after often severe and prolonged fighting, in the spring. The male's behaviour during copulation, which is prolonged, is peculiarly aggressive; he often seizes the female by the head and holds her in his jaws for a long time, a practice also indulged in by mating crocodiles. The slow-worm is ovo-viviparous. The young are born in membranous sacks. Young slow-worms are abundant in early September – a good place to look for them is under stones, logs or old pieces of corrugated iron. They are very different from the adults, being much lighter in colour, pale cream almost, with the black vertebral stripe clearly defined. They are also somehow far more serpentine in appearance and movement. The first time I caught young slow-worms, when I was young and a snake-snob, I infinitely preferred them to their adult relatives.

The adjective *fragilis* refers to the tail, ending in a needle-sharp point. This is almost as breakable as the tail of the common lizard. Be careful of it when you handle the creature. Slow-worms struggle frantically at first when caught and have an unpleasant habit of opening their vents and excreting over your fingers. Like lizards, they 'tame' in a matter of minutes and you can almost swear that they get to know you. They will bite, though, if provoked. One of my childhood companions, of a rather fanciful disposition, caught two slow-worms and persuaded them to bite the lobes of his ears. They hung on tight and he arrived home wearing a pair of live slow-worm earrings; not very well received.

In captivity the slow-worm thrives quietly, if properly treated. Care must be taken when exhibiting it to the herpetologically ignorant, especially rustics. Even today, it is very difficult to persuade them that it is not venomous. They are convinced that its needle-pointed tail is a string. Only a few years ago a gravedigger in a Surrey village 20 miles from London assured me that his churchyard had been infested – until he decimated them with his scythe – with little red stinging death adders. No wonder *Anguis fragilis* is secretive in its habits. Apart from ignorant men, its predators include vipers, hedgehogs, grass snakes, rats and hawks. It is, however, the most long-lived of lizards. One has been reported from the Copenhagen Museum which had arrived when adult and lived there for fifty-four years. At the age of forty-five it mated with a female at least twenty years old.

Early reports that the European green lizard (*Lacerta viridis*) and the wall lizard (*Lacerta muralis*), both of which inhabit the Channel Islands, had been found in southern England are probably due either to confusion with the sand lizards in the breeding season or to escapes from vivaria. But attempts to introduce both these beautiful species into suitable parts of southern England have been at any rate partly successful. A colony of green lizards was installed in the Isle of

Wight in 1899 and is known to have bred there, but they have not been seen since 1936. Four colonies of wall lizard introduced into Surrey and the Isle of Wight 20 years ago are still thriving and have bred, but there is no likelihood of their spreading. The British lizard-student must confine his attention to the three native species. They afford him a perhaps unexpected amount of variety.

Chapter 5

The Marvellous Chamaeleon

For me the chamaeleon is the most fascinating reptile of them all. It seems to move like one in a dream who is obeying a spell. Everything about it is in some way fantastic and pleasing. It combines beauty with grotesquerie. How did this slow-moving, highly specialised arboreal form with its unique features evolve from the agamids which are, with this one exception, all fast-moving, thrusting, darting lizards? We do not know. All we can do is to speculate and make tautologous statements such as 'chamaeleons are specially adapted for living among vegetation on a diet of insects'.

The unique features are the swivel eyes which can move independently and cover a wide field of vision and are protected by scaly turrets; the tongue with its adhesive pad which can be shot out to a distance of many inches and brought back instantly into the mouth with the prey sticking to it; and the arrangement of the toes in opposed groups of two and three, peculiarly apt for grasping thin branches and stalks. The ability to change colour, and the prehensile tail, are found in other lizards, though perhaps not quite so highly developed. But also unique is the slow deliberation of all chamaeleonid movements except for the swivelling of the eye-turrets and the high-speed sharpshooting, faster than the human eye can follow, of the tongue. (The nearest approach to the chamaeleon's gait is found, as Bellairs points out, in that odd little arboreal mammal the loris.)

Some other agamids use their tongues for catching prey, but the chamaeleons have brought it to a fine art. At full stretch the tongue is as long as the body and tail together, or even longer, with a lobed tip which becomes adhesive by the secretion of mucous glands. It can

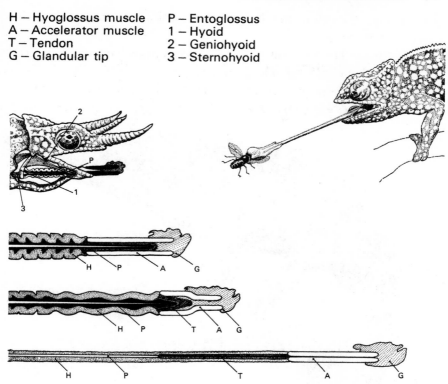

H – Hyoglossus muscle
A – Accelerator muscle
T – Tendon
G – Glandular tip

P – Entoglossus
1 – Hyoid
2 – Geniohyoid
3 – Sternohyoid

be shot out in one twenty-fifth of a second. It is in the form of a tube with muscular walls and when withdrawn it folds up concertina-wise.

The family *Chamaeleonidae* is reasonably flourishing and is probably in more danger from men of all races and colours than from natural predators. Camouflage is supplemented by the chamaeleon's immobility. Predators rely a great deal on movement to stimulate their sight; indeed some snakes' eyes don't seem to take in an object until it moves. Another feature which helps the camouflage is the way the body is flattened, from side to side, giving it extra resemblance to a leaf.

There are eighty-one species, all in the Old World. Nearly half of these live in Africa and nearly half, again, in Madagascar. One small species lives on the shores of the Mediterranean from Palestine westward to North Africa and southern Spain. There is one species in

India, one in Ceylon and one in the south-western corner of the Arabian peninsula.

Size varies. The smallest species, the common chamaeleon, is little more than 3 inches long. The giant *Chamaeleo oustaleti* of Madagascar is 22 inches. There are several fine large East African chamaeleons; one species, Jackson's chamaeleon, has three large horns on its nose.

Jackson's chamaeleon *(Chamaeleon jacksoni)*

These, whatever purpose they may serve, give it a slightly unbalanced – I mean aesthetically, not emotionally – appearance; I find them somehow faintly displeasing. More elegant is the type of headgear – a neatly designed, not too elaborate casque-style helmet – sported by the common chamaeleon.

The colour changes can be striking, though not quite so sensational as in those not-so-funny stories told by saloon-bar wits about chamaeleons exploding when placed on tartan kilts. Most chamaeleons are green, generally a fairly bright green. They can pass from this to a pale yellow or a dark brown. The spots, which are mostly black, may temporarily disappear. The pigment cells which affect the colour changes can be stimulated locally by applied light, and experiments have shown that it makes no difference if you blindfold the chamaeleon. It behaves in fact as if it had skin-sight.

The prehensile tail is delightfully specialised with the skin well padded with muscle and raised on the lower side in flexible scaly spines that are perfect for gripping; flexibility is one of the keynotes in chamaeleon design.

Chamaeleons in good health are voracious, almost continuous eaters. They are almost entirely insectivorous, though one giant Madagascar chamaeleon was observed by Inger to snap up with its tongue a half-grown mouse at a range of about a foot. The appearance of quiet concentration with which a chamaeleon, when it has spotted a fly with one of its eyes, turns its head to bring both eyes to bear, and with them its stereoscopic vision which gives the range for the tongue, is most impressive. One must be careful not to credit them with too much intelligence. The following instance, recorded by Inger, may help to correct for anthropomorphism. A captive chamaeleon shot at an earthworm in a dish of water and because of the moisture its tongue failed to stick. It moved half an inch nearer and shot again. The process was repeated again and again until the chamaeleon got in so close that it took the worm in its jaws.

The horns on the various horned species are much more developed in males than females. They do not appear ever to be used, certainly not in fighting. There is some fighting at the breeding season, but it is of the ritual bluff variety. The males distend their bodies with air and hiss; that is all. During fights, whether over females or territory, the males change colour; the loser turns a dull greyish-brown (skinheads might well copy this civilised example).

Most species are egg-laying; a few are viviparous and never need to descend from the cover of the leafy branches. The egg-laying females dig sizeable holes in which to lay the eggs; they fill the holes in afterwards and press the earth down with their hindfeet. Most species lay from twenty to forty eggs; incubation may take six weeks or more. The viviparous species, many of them South African, deposit their young in their membranes on convenient twigs, and they struggle out and cling on.

Chamaeleons unquestionably have a social life, but again we must be careful not to credit them with too much intelligence. The spectacle of a female chamaeleon on a branch, with her young ones trying out their prehensile tails on twigs close by, is likely to touch off tender sentiments; but photographs of it in books by herpetologists are generally given a warning caption: 'This does not imply parental care.'[1]

The established facts are unfortunately scanty. Courtship has been observed. The males perform a series of head jerks, like agamids. Eventually the male, at first still anchored by the tip of its tail to a branch, clambers on top of the female and grips her round the body, his forelimbs round her neck and his hindlimbs round her waist so that she is compelled to take him for a ride. In colonies of chamaeleons in captivity males will stake out their own little territories and challenge male intruders; females are permitted. There are also certain 'butch' females which resemble males in appearance and behave with the utmost aggressiveness.

The age of chamaeleons is a subject of controversy. Most reptiles have a comparatively long span of life. Why should the chamaeleon have the shortest span of any? Yet very few chamaeleons in captivity (this is also discussed on p. 166) live for more than two years and none for more than three. This applies even to the chamaeleons in che Giza Zoological Gardens at Cairo where conditions were supposed to be ideal. Opponents of the short-span theory maintain that chamaeleons are so special that no artificial conditions ever really suit them.

[1] Some herpetologists are so cautious that they write this on their Christmas cards.

the Amazonian tree boa, grows to a length of six feet and has the largest front teeth of any nonvenomous species.

Chapter 6

The Snakes:

Suborder *Serpentes*

First, inevitably, some elementary classification. There are close on 3000 species divided into ten main families. One of these, the *Colubridae*, contains more than 2000 species. There are, of course, many genera.

I am beginning with the more primitive snakes and working upwards towards the most advanced.

FAMILY TYPHLOPIDAE. These are the blind or worm snakes, a group of burrowers of about 180 species. They are all very small, between 9 inches and 2 feet. Their eyes are rudimentary. They eat insects, mostly termites. They are widely distributed over the warm parts of the Old and New Worlds and Australia. They are thought to be an aberrant form or offshoot not closely related to the main line of evolutionary descent. All their teeth are in the upper jaw.

FAMILY LEPTOTYPHLOPIDAE. Another family of some forty burrowers, slimmer than the above, sometimes called the thread snakes. Their distribution is very similar to that of the blind snakes. They have teeth in the lower jaw only.

FAMILY ANILIIDAE. These are both burrowers and non-burrowers thought to be nearer the main line of descent. Distribution: Asia and South America. There are three quite varied subfamilies as follows:

Subfamily *Aniliinae*: including the pipe snakes. The Malayan pipe snake has a trick, shared by many snakes of quite different families, of cocking up the scarlet tip of its tail as if to distract attention from its head or to attract prey.

Subfamily *Uropeltinae*: the rough tails, so called because of the spiny tail.

Subfamily *Xenopeltinae*: this comprises one species only, *Xenopeltis unicolor*, the sunbeam snake, which is sometimes given a family to itself.

Like the boas it has two lungs but no traces of limbs or pelvis. It is about 3 feet long and its skin is iridescent in sunlight. It inhabits South-east Asia.

FAMILY ACROCHORDIDAE. There seems to be some controversy about this family, which is sometimes described as a subfamily of the *Colubridae* but is, perhaps more authoritatively, classed as a separate family. Distribution is in India, South-east Asia, New Guinea and northern Australia. There are two species, the elephant's trunk snake (*Acrochordus javanicus*) and the file snake. The elephant's trunk snake grows to a length of 6 feet and is very thick in the body. It is aquatic and nocturnal, has valved nostrils and small eyes. It stays under water for long periods and swims well but slowly. On land it is out of

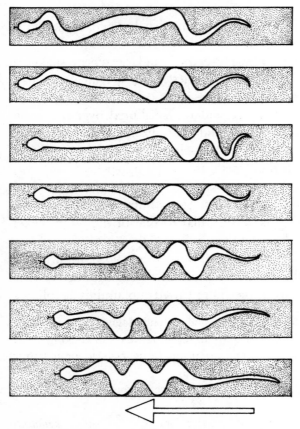

Diagram of concertina movement of snake in confined space

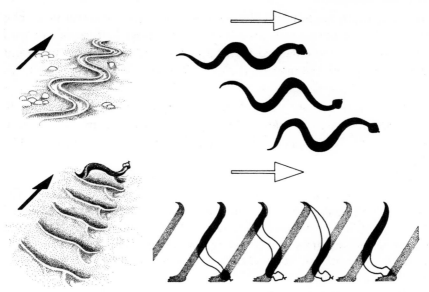

Diagram of (A) undulating and (B) sidewinding progression of snakes

place. The file snake is half the size and almost entirely marine, with a flattened tail.

FAMILY BOIDAE. This important family of 100 and more species contains the world's largest and some of its smallest snakes: the huge reticulated python of Malaya and the anaconda of South America, and the tiny sand boas. Subfamilies are:

Subfamily *Erysinae*: distribution North America, North Africa, West Africa. These are small, burrowing and secretive. They include the sand boas.

Subfamily *Pythoninae*: the pythons; distribution mainly in the Old World and Australia; mostly oviparous.

Subfamily *Boinae*: distribution New World and Madagascar. Mostly viviparous.

FAMILY COLUBRIDAE. Nearly 2000 species widely distributed in the Old and New Worlds. These are the typical snakes. Most of them are non-venomous, though there are venomous species: back-fanged snakes; most of these are only mildly venomous, but there are some dangerous exceptions.

The *Colubridae* have no traces of legs or pelvic girdles, and only one lung. The bones of the skull, except those surrounding the brain, are loosely articulated and the jaws capable of wide distension. The lower jaw consists of only two bones. The upper surface of the head is covered by nine enlarged plates and there is a circular transparent scale, the 'spectacle' covering the eye. When the skin is being cast this looks like a blue film.

The *Colubridae* vary a good deal in size, from 2 feet to 12 feet in some species; also in habits. Some are climbers; some are ground snakes; some are aquatic. There are a number of subfamilies. The largest is:

Subfamily *Colubrinae*: there are very many species. They include the fast-moving land snakes of both Old and New Worlds known as racers, generally feeding on rodents or lizards; the English smooth snake (*Coronella austriaca*) and the grass snake (*Natrix natrix*) are well-known colubrines; so are the Aesculapian snake (*Elaphe longissima*) and the four-lined snake (*Elaphe quatuor lineata*).

There are several other smaller but interesting subfamilies of the *Colubridae*. Among them are:

Subfamily *Dipsadinae*, known as the thirst snakes, comprising about seventy species distributed over South-east Asia and Central America. They are small snakes around 3 feet long, mainly nocturnal, with large eyes. Their jaws are specially adapted for eating slugs and snails; the long lower jaw works its way inside the shell and winkles out the snail. (The ancients believed they were deadly; they are, of course, perfectly harmless.

Subfamily *Dasypeltinae*: distribution mainly in Africa with one Indian species. These small snakes are specially adapted for eating eggs and commonly known as the egg-eating snakes. Many snakes will eat eggs, but the *Dasypeltinae* have a unique arrangement by which spines on some of the vertebrae press down on the gullet and break the shell, which is then spat out. The teeth are poorly developed. An egg-eating snake only 3 feet long can manage a hen's egg. In the process of engulfing the egg before it is broken the jaws become temporarily dislocated and the skin stretched to an unusual extent.

There are many species of venomous *Colubridae*. Most of them belong to the Suborder *Boiginae*. Their distribution is fairly wide in the Old and New Worlds. These are the back-fanged snakes. They have several enlarged teeth at the back of the jaw down which the venom dribbles from the venom gland as they bite. One species, *Malpolon monspessulana*, is found in southern Europe, including parts of France where it is known by the imposing name of '*Le Grand Couleuvre de Montpellier*'. It is in fact the largest snake in Europe with a record length of 6 feet 6 inches. It is light brown, slender, a rodent-eater, mostly ground-moving but capable of climbing after birds. Its venom has a mild but quite distinct effect on man.

Several of the *Boiginae* are tree snakes. The most venomous of them is *Dispholidus typus*, the South African boomslange, a long, slender, beautiful green snake. The venom of the *Boiginae* acts on the

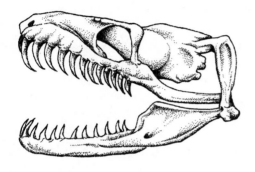

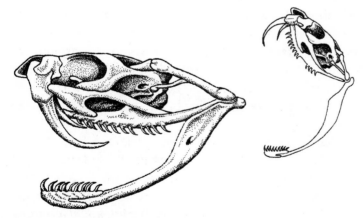

Top: Skull of nonvenomous snake

Bottom: Skull of venomous snake showing fangs, folded and erect

nervous centres and is chemically similar to that of the elapids; but judging by the symptoms of K. P. Schmidt, the American herpetologist who died of a boomslange's bite, it also affects the blood.

The poison-fang apparatus of the *Boiginae* is inefficient compared with that of the cobras and even more so compared with that of the vipers. Most back-fanged snakes need to chew several times before the fangs can go into action. The boomslange, however, strikes with its mouth wide open, which is probably one of the reasons why it has caused the deaths of a number of human beings. Curiously enough, the most developed boigine fangs are found among the smaller burrowing species, in which the jaw bone is short and the fangs quite far forward. There are several eccentric developments among the *Boiginae*. The long-nosed tree snake of South and Central Africa, excessively slender and bright leaf-green, is expert at camouflage, and its strange turned-up snout can easily be mistaken for a leaf. An even weirder back-fanged snake is the leaf-nosed snake of Madagascar (*Langaha intermedia*), 3 feet long and brown in colour. In the females the snout is protracted into a fantastic leaf-like appendage; in the males it is a simple conical point.

The most remarkable member of this group is the flying snake (*Chrysopelea ornata*) of Indonesia, India and Ceylon. This, known as the golden flying tree-snake – there is actually more than one species of this strange genus – may be bright green with yellow or red spots; it is quite small, about 3 feet, entirely arboreal and mainly a lizard-eater. It is not only a most accomplished climber but it can glide through the air from branch to branch or down to the ground. It does this by holding its body rigid and spreading its ribs and drawing in its belly so that its lower surface becomes slightly concave. Possibly gliding is a slight exaggeration, but it most certainly parachutes.

Another remarkable member of the *Boiginae* is the large South American species, *Pseudoboa cloelia*, the mussurana, 8 feet long, which preys on the highly venomous *fer de lance,* one of the largest of the New World viperines, overpowers it with ease and gobbles it up. Also curious are the fishing snakes, especially *Herpeton tentaculatum* from Indo-China. This has two tentacles on its nose which it waves about under water to lure the fish within striking distance.

The remaining three groups are all poisonous.

Subfamily *Elapidae*: some 150 species comprising the cobras and kraits of Africa and India; the mambas of Africa; the venomous snakes of the Americas; and several exceedingly poisonous snakes of Australia. Nearly all are oviparous. The elapids are colubrid in type but have fangs at the front of the jaws. The fangs are relatively short compared to the long needle-like fangs of the vipers. In some species the venom flows down a groove in the outside of the fang; in others the groove has closed up to form a channel.

Subfamily *Hydrophiidae*: the sea snakes. About fifty species have been discovered, though there may be many more. Mainly found in South-east Asian seas and the Indian Ocean. These snakes are of medium size, up to 8 feet, and marvels of adaptation, with specially flattened tails and bodies for swimming, very large single lungs and valves in their nostrils. Some species can't move on land at all. Their venom is neurotoxic like that of the elapids, and potent. The fangs are of the open-groove type. They are described in some detail in Chapter 8.

There remains the family of the *Viperidae*, containing more than eighty species. These, which include the subfamilies of *Viperinae* — the true vipers of the Old World — and the subfamily of *Crotalidae*, comprising the rattlesnakes, bushmasters, and tree-climbing vipers, are described in Chapter 9. They are often called the pit vipers because of the little sensory pit between their eyes and their nostrils.

Chapter 7

Pythons and Boas

Sensationalism, like greed and all perversions of appetite, is habit-forming and very dangerous; indeed it may yet destroy us all. We get an example of it when we consider the big snakes, the pythons and the boas. The largest python (*Python reticulatus*) of Indonesia reaches a length of 33 feet. The largest boa, the anaconda of Brazil (*Eunectes murinus*), is 29 feet. You would think these surely generous proportions might satisfy. Not so. The myth of stupendous serpents never dies. And it sometimes gets a shot in the tail from unexpectedly strange characters. That eccentric traveller, Major Fawcett, for instance. He was supposed to be carrying out a survey for the Royal Geographical Society in Amazonia, but you might have thought he was writing a serial for the *News of the World*. I wish I knew more about this odd figure. He seems to have been rather melancholy but perhaps this was the depressive phase. The tribe of Munchausen are generally cheerful megalomaniacs. Anyway, in his diary he, or somebody, wrote that in April 1907 he had shot an anaconda 62 feet long.[1] He went on to embroider the story: 'A penetrating foetid odour emanated from the snake, probably its breath which is believed to have a stupefying effect, first attacking and later paralysing the prey.' This rubbish reads like the work of some whisky-inflamed hack in a bar in EC4.

However, there were giant serpents in the Eocene fifty to sixty million years ago, that would have made even *P. reticulatus* and *E.*

[1] About the same time Bram Stoker, resting on *Dracula's* laurels, was writing *The Lair of the White Worm*, about an ancient and noble English family persecuted by a giant snake 200 feet long that lived at the bottom of a well in the deerpark. The Chinese, some thousand years earlier, had gone a few steps further with a python that could swallow an elephant and pass the bones and tusks three years later.

murenus look like grass snakes. One whose fossil remains exist was *Gigantophis*, possibly 50 feet long, inhabiting Egypt; another was a South American denizen; but there is no certainty here because palaeontologists are not agreed about the deductions that can be drawn from the fossil vertebrae. It is possible that there is a maximum length beyond which a snake becomes unviable.

This one family, the *Boidae*, comprising the pythons and the boas, is always the most popular with the general public. The beautifully coloured and patterned iridescent skins, graceful bodies and shapely intelligent-seeming heads of the *Boidae* — never mind for the moment about the degenerate burrowing forms, some of which are distressingly hideous — seem to instil confidence. Here, says the little subtopian hominid, is a healthy snake. Yet it is a safe bet that every one of us has some remote simian relation who was seized, constricted and swallowed, after dying quickly but with a shrill scream of terror, by an ancestral python or boa. They are great monkey eaters. Kipling,[1] though his zoology was often inaccurate, had got to the heart of the matter when he portrayed the bandar-log as terrified of the python. Desmond Morris describes how, following the experiments of Haslerud at the Yerkes Ape Colony in America, he tested a young male chimpanzee.

The little ape was slightly scared of a piece of rubber tubing but soon began to play with it. It was taken away and returned to him with zig-zag markings painted on it. The chimpanzee was terrified. He 'retreated, then advanced with all his hair on end and dealt it a vicious blow behind its "head", then leapt back out of the way'. A mechanical snake 'that wriggled realistically' was offered: the chimpanzee fled screaming. 'He would only return when it had stopped moving. Then he flicked it away as hard as he could.'

[1] I have never been able to understand why Kipling had such a down on monkeys, especially when he himself was so apish and imitative. Did he perhaps identify them with some 'inferior' race, the voluble Hindus, or with anarchist intellectuals? There are strange undercurrents in the sociology of Mowgli's jungle. Bagheera and Baloo and even Kaa, the rock python, are like prefects or housemasters, Mowgli and the young wolves the boys. But the poor bandar-log don't belong, and it is hinted that they have vices from which decent animals are free. As R. M. Dawkins used to say: Kipling wrote about a public school like a jungle and a jungle like a public school.

Gradually he plucked up courage and picked it up, but very cautiously and always by the tip of the tail. 'It was hard to believe,' writes Morris, 'that he was not a seasoned snake-hunter. In fact he had been caught as a tiny baby several years before.' This suggests an instinctive fear of small poisonous snakes. As for two young orangutans, both reared in captivity and typically lethargic, 'when they saw a tame python in a television studio . . . they were up the wall and into the studio rigging quicker than they had ever moved in their lives'.

The *Boidae* are an interesting blend of the advanced and the primitive. They have vestiges of the pelvis and of hindlimbs which can be observed in some species in the form of little spurs, quite conspicuous in the males. They have well-developed lungs, whereas the advanced snakes, the colubrids and vipers, have lost all pelvic vestiges and their left lungs are suppressed, with the right ones elongated. At the same time the *Boidae* have several features of the advanced snakes: wide mobile jaws, big ventral scales and — except for the burrowing forms —well-developed eyes. The main difference between the two subfamilies is that the boas have no supraorbital bone in the roofs of their mouths and are viviparous, whereas the pythons are all egg-layers. In their geographical distribution there is a fairly sharp division. All pythons inhabit the Old World including Australasia; most boas the New World.

In the great subfamily of *Pythoninae* there are seven species which are considered the pythons 'pure', the Vere de Veres. We may as well begin with the biggest.

Python reticulatus, the reticulated python of South-east Asia, the East Indies and the Philippines, grows to a length of 33 feet, though the average is much less. (It is sometimes called the regal python, though slight confusion may arise here because there is also an African royal python. Perhaps in the future it may be renamed the Chairman Mao python.) It is quite slender and weighs less, foot for foot, than the Indian rock python or the anaconda. Its head is brown with a black line along the centre. Its body is light brown with black markings like a network. It eats a variety of mammals, some quite small. The largest prey that even a quite big specimen is likely to swallow is a pig. The last *P. reticulatus* I saw was a sizeable specimen of at least 16 feet who was swallowing a dead rabbit and taking its time about it. Its danger to man has been much exaggerated. There is, however, according to Schmidt and Inger, an authenticated case of a reticulated python swallowing a fourteen-year-old Malayan boy on the island of Salebabu.

It is mainly a forest-dweller and is fond of water, but it has a strange penchant for the haunts of men. In 1899, according to the naturalist Major Stanley, reticulated pythons were quite common in the suburbs of Bangkok and along the banks of the Menam river. Here, 'oblivious of steamers and junks unloading . . . rice-mill chimneys filling the air with smoke and hundreds of noisy coolies . . . he selects some hole or crevice in a building, timber stack or bank to spend the day in, and at night makes an easy living devouring fowls, ducks, cats, dogs, and, it is said, pigs . . . in 1897 a python was found in the King's palace.' (According to Crompton it was cut open and found to have swallowed one of the royal Siamese cats, which was identified by a silver bell.)

One's first reaction to this might be that Major Stanley should have been seconded to the Horse Marines along with Major Fawcett. One would be wrong. Major Stanley was an accurate observer. And *P. reticulatus'* liking for dockside life has often led to his stowing away in ships. One adventurer fetched up in London and was handed over to the Reptile House. It is, like most pythons, a splendid swimmer and often puts out to sea. In 1888 when the island of Krakatoa went up in a volcanic eruption bigger than an H-bomb explosion, refugee pythons were said to have landed on the coasts of Java and Sumatra.

P. reticulatus lays up to 82 eggs in a clutch. The female pushes them into a heap and coils round them, managing to raise the temperature considerably. Incubation takes about eighty days.

A python's power depends to a great extent on its mechanical situation and whether it can get any purchase for its coils. Four men, one at the head, one at the end of the tail, one at the anus and one in between it and the head, can hold a 20-foot python without too much trouble. Kipling's description of Kaa, the rock python, battering down a wall with a blow from his head is, as has often been pointed out, complete invention. A python when it strikes makes a snatching movement to fasten its jaws on its prey. Irritable pythons in zoos sometimes strike at the glass in the vain hope of biting the public; they retire with bloody noses and have to be nursed by their keepers.

The Indian rock python, *Python molurus*, is stronger and sturdier than *P. reticulatus*. (A 19-foot specimen weighed 200 lbs as compared with a *P. reticulatus* 28 feet long which weighed 250 lbs.) Its maximum length is 25 feet. It has a dark mark on the head like a spear point. There are two subspecies probably, certainly two phases of body coloration. In one the skin is dark olive with blackish markings; in the other, which inhabits western India, the background skin is palish grey and the markings dark tan with a pinkish tinge about the head. There is a good deal of difference between the two variations (named, by Werner, *intermedia* and *ocellata*). *Ocellata*, the lighter one, has a charming friendly disposition. This is the python for pet's playtime, or showbiz, the stripteaser's friend.

P. molurus is found outside India, from West Pakistan to South China, and should really be called the Asiatic rock python. It likes water and can stay under for quite a time. It eats pigs and small deer, ducks, pheasants and peacock. Its strength as a constrictor must be very great, for the remains of a leopard were taken from the stomach of an 18-foot python, the wounds on whose skin were quite slight. The python's initial striking bite which it makes at any convenient part of its prey may be quite severe. The coils are then thrown round the body of the prey so quickly that the human eye often cannot follow the movement.

Like most snakes pythons take a lot of killing. Captain Smith of the Indian Forest Service (quoted by John Crompton) was walking with his spaniel. It ran on ahead. Yelps were heard. Smith rushed up and found his dog in the coils of an 11-foot python. He beat it savagely with a heavy stick; it unloosed its coils and released the dog. Smith's bearers went on beating the python until they thought it was dead and then lugged it back to camp and laid it out ready for skinning. Smith was having a drink and congratulating his dog on its escape when a boy rushed into his tent. The python had disappeared. It was caught trying to make off with a chicken.

Python curtus, called the blood python because of its hue, like that of rather cloudy gore, is a much smaller species found in Indonesia.

It is thick in the body, with a short tail, and is an expert rat-catcher.

The African python, *Python sebae* (named after Albert Seba, the eighteenth-century naturalist whose work was used by Linnaeus as a basis for his system of animal classification), is found in most of Africa south of the Sahara. It is a big snake, nearly if not quite as long as the Indian rock python and of powerful build, yellowish, with dark mottled markings, rather darker than the Asiatic python. This is the python of antiquity, the Serpent of Old Nile. A huge specimen from the upper reaches of the Nile took part in the processions in honour of Dionysus in Alexandria. This is probably the snake described by Virgil in the Aeneid. (See p. 173.)

P. sebae in the wild is naturally savage. There is an authenticated record of its having attacked an African woman washing by the bank of a river. This python was 14 feet long, too small to swallow any woman — except possibly Gagool. In captivity it becomes quite docile. *P. sebae* plays an important part in African folklore and is often eaten, more for reasons of sympathetic magic than gourmandise, though its flesh is quite palatable, like toughish veal.

Python regius, the royal python of West Africa, is quite small, little more than 5 feet with subtly mottled beige and dark mauve markings. This is a dear little python with a most gentle disposition and a genuinely pleasing personality. In the wild it has, like several other species, an interesting trick of curling itself into a tight round ball with its head tucked inside, but in captivity it becomes so tame that it cannot be induced to perform this protective exercise.

Over to Australia. The Australian python which has been renamed *Morelia argus* and given a genus to itself, has bright yellow spots on each of its scales and diamond-shaped dark markings on a yellow background. Its maximum length is 12 feet. It feeds on the usual small-mammal diet. Before myxamytosis it was popular with farmers because it kept down the rabbit population. It is an all-round athlete, arboreal and aquatic.

There is another quite distinct group of Australian rock pythons, of the genus *Liasis*, found in northern Australia, Timor, New Guinea and the Philippines. *L. amethystinus*, inhabiting the mangrove clumps of northern Australia, eats opossums and has been known to reach a length of 20 feet. The head shields are larger than those of the 'pure' pythons. Yet another small group, the aspidites (nothing to do with vipers), called *woma* by the aborigines, is popular locally because it eats venomous snakes.

One of the most beautiful of all the Australasian snakes is the green tree python of New Guinea (*Chrondropython viridis*), vivid leaf green with white spots (the young are brick red, later yellow). This is an arboreal snake with a prehensile tail and big front teeth, all the better for coping with fast-moving prey. Its maximum length is 7 feet. It has affinities with the New World tree boas.

The African burrowing python (*Calabaria rheinhardti*), ranging from West Africa to the Congo, 3 feet long, has some of the marks of degeneration that go with subterranean life: cylindrical body, small narrow head, short tail, smooth scales. It is dark brown with some pink on the sides. It too rolls itself into a ball, and it cocks up its tail. Though totally inoffensive and never biting, it is dreaded by the natives who think it has two heads.

Now for the *Boidae*. No reason really, though it is perhaps not so

Anaconda *(Eunectes murinus)*

typical as some, why we should not begin with their King, the anaconda, of the swampy river beds of tropical South America, the Orinoco and the Amazon and their tributaries. Its length, we have seen, is a matter of dispute. The British Zoological Society credits it with a maximum of 29 feet. The New York Zoological Society's prize of $5000 for a 30 foot specimen has not yet been won. Its colour is dark olive green with black spots. It is a bulkier snake than the reticulated python. It is strong enough, though there is something faintly displeasing about its proportions which do not give you the impression of an all-round athlete. Though semi-aquatic it is not quite in the top flight as a swimmer by the highest ophidian standards. It lurks in shallow swamps waiting for prey and is a crafty stalker, swimming under birds and dragging them down. It eats the South American mammals, tapirs, peccaries, capybaras, and sometimes young crocodilians. After a kill it may leave a broad trail in the mud and this has helped to perpetuate the myth of the giant anaconda. Viviparous, it produces large litters; seventy-two at a birth have been recorded. The young are about 2 feet long, delightful little things. The anaconda does reasonably well in captivity, though the temperament of full-grown specimens is liable to be uncertain.

The boa-constrictor of Central and South America (*Constrictor constrictor*) is a more beautiful snake, a good deal smaller. The record is 18 feet, but the average is 10–12 feet. It is marked with a complicated pattern of dark brown diamonds inset with white on a background of creamy beige. Young boa-constrictors tame easily, and they do well in captivity and have lived for 25 years. Some of the Central American variations are notoriously bad-tempered and, like many snakes, infested with ticks.

Several species of boa are found in the Caribbean islands. A particularly fine athletic example is the Cuban boa (*Epicrates angulifer*), also found on the Isle of Pines. It is about 12 feet long, beautifully slender, arboreal and mainly nocturnal, feeding on bats and rats. It has labial sensory pits which probably help it in tracking them. A relation is the rainbow boa (*Epicrates cenchris*) found between the south of Mexico and northern Argentina. Its scales have a peculiar iridescent quality although the background colour is quite sober. It is part ground-dweller, part arboreal. A lesser-known genus of ground boas is called *Tropidophis*. A Cuban species, *T. semicunctus*, only 16 inches long, bleeds at the mouth when angry, and its eyes turn red.

Among other notable South American boas is the emerald tree boa (*Boa canina*), brilliant green with a white line down its back. It has a habit of coiling neatly round a branch with its head resting between coils. It is quite small, not more than 4 feet. This is the gentlest of the tree boas, some of which can be very nasty and have unusually long fang-like (entirely nonvenomous, of course) teeth. The most interesting and evil-tempered of them all is Cook's boa (*Boa enydris cookii*), which is a delicious golden sandy brown. Arboreal, bird-eating and very slender, it is a brilliant climber and can scale a vertical bamboo pole.

Outside Central and South America there are a few scattered boa species. There are three in Madagascar. One of these, *Sanginia madagascarensis*, is particularly closely related to the New World tree boas, an example of the convergence of species. On Round Island near Mauritius there are two odd little quasi-boas classed in a genus of their own, *bolyeria*. They have no pelvic vestiges, but they have spines on their posterior vertebrae and – a unique feature – an additional joint on the maxillary bone. On the main island of Mauritius they were liquidated by the wild pigs, the same barbarian tribe who finished off the last dodo.

In some Pacific islands – Fiji and Samoa – there are small boas of the Papuan genus *Enygrus*. One of these, *Enygrus asper schmidti*, is named after the late Dr Karl Schmidt. It has a rather viperine appearance and temperament. Dr Schmidt records, from the same voyage on which he discovered his *enygrus*, an amusing misunderstanding from the Marquesas. Neither there nor in Tahiti are there any snakes. Yet rumours were going of serpents, possibly of preternatural subtlety, on the islands. They were due, it transpired, to a missionary's translation into Polynesian of the Book of Genesis.

In North America there are three small boas. The rosy boa (*Lichanura roseofusca*) is found in California and western Arizona, also *L. trivugata*, both about 3 feet long, and mouse-eating. The rubber boa or silver boa of the western USA and southern Canada is a very small burrower whose defence is to hide its head in its coils and raise and wriggle its tail.

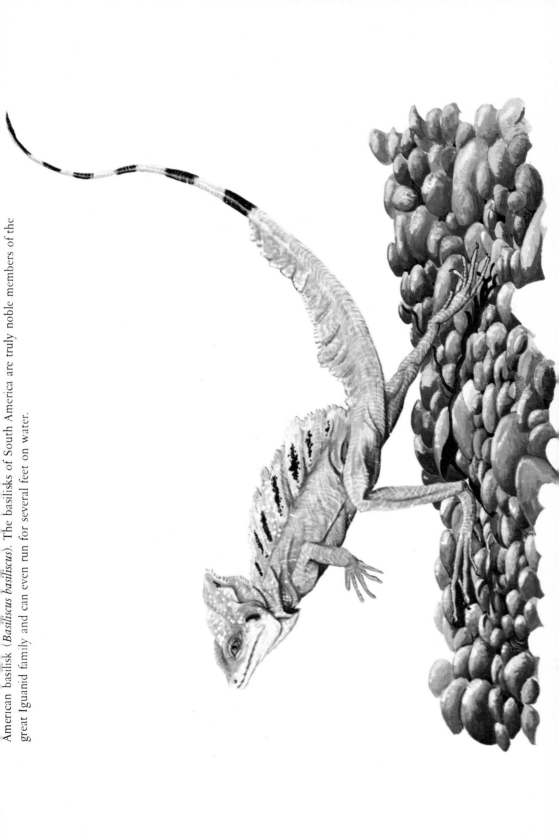

American basilisk (*Basiliscus basiliscus*). The basilisks of South America are truly noble members of the great Iguanid family and can even run for several feet on water.

In the Old World there are seven species of small burrowing sand boas, mostly in North Africa and the Middle East, though one species is found north of the Himalayas and in north-western China and another in north-eastern India. Typical species are *Eryx jaculus*, the spotted sand boa of north-eastern Africa and western Asia, also

Striped whipsnake *(Coluber taeniatus)*

found in southern Europe; and *Eryx johnii*, the brown sand boa of India with a burrower's snout and a tail so blunt that it is often called the two-headed snake. A stranger form is that of *Gongylophis conicus*, also Indian, nearly 3 feet long, with a bloated body and some pain- fully rough scales towards the tail.

Chapter 8

Venomous Snakes

The *Elapidae*: cobras and kraits; mambas; the
Australians; coral snakes; sea snakes

The peculiar glamour attaching to venomous snakes used to be
expressed in nineteenth-century herpetological circles by the splendid word *thanatophidia* (death-serpents), which was used to denote
them all irrespective of classification. Let us look more closely at
some of them, beginning with the *Elapidae*.

Their king is *Naja hannah*, the hamadryad, or king cobra, a
superb snake which grows to the length, truly sensational for a
venomous species, of 18 feet 9 inches. Sometimes it is given a special
genus of its own, *Ophiophagus* on account of its cannibalistic habits.
The hamadryad is a strong shapely snake with a quite slender body.
A 15-foot specimen in the New York Zoo was $2\frac{1}{2}$ inches in diameter,
a great deal less than that of a python of equal length. Its colour
varies between olive and yellowish brown with crossbands of black.
Sometimes there is an orange tint about the throat and chin. The
belly is pale. The hood, though not quite so wide in proportion when
spread as that of the Indian cobra, is impressive. Some people remark
on the intensity of the hamadryad's stare. It certainly looks alert, as
if it were taking notice of its surroundings. Reputation apart, there
is nothing particularly sinister about its appearance. Indeed, the
expressions on the faces of a courting couple, with the male lightly
flicking his forked tongue over the female's head, can easily be
construed as idyllic. Who knows? Perhaps they are.

The hamadryad is found, though not abundantly, in parts of India,
in Burma, Siam, southern China and South-east Asia including the
Philippines. It is more diurnal in its habits than the ordinary Indian
cobra. Its diet consists entirely of other snakes and sometimes smaller
members of its own species; but there seems to be doubt about

whether it will take venomous snakes. Ditmars maintains it can discriminate between venomous and nonvenomous species. One large specimen in captivity fed regularly once a week, averaging four snakes a meal. A natural all-round athlete, it can climb and swim expertly. It seems to do everything with a style and *élan* of its own. But a hamadryad is no match for a constrictor. According to Crompton, in a fight in Burma between a 10-foot hamadryad and an 8-foot python the hamadryad was getting the worst of it. The python had made a deep tear in the hamadryad's side and had coiled all round it . . . but 'at this interesting stage some coolies killed both snakes'.

Everybody who has had anything to do with hamadryads will tell you they are the most intelligent of all snakes, in a class by themselves. Captive specimens soon learn not to strike against the glass fronts of their cages. Ditmars thinks they get to recognize the people who feed them and look after them while remaining hostile to strangers. When feeding time rolls round they will peer through cracks watching for the keeper. Rudolf Meyer de Schauense of the Academy of Natural Sciences of Philadelphia records an impressive story of a hamadryad quickly learning to drink from 'the nozzle of a pitcher'.

The hamadryad is the only snake that can be said to make – build is perhaps hardly the word – a nest. The female winds loops of her body round dead leaves and rotting vegetation and draws them up into a mound, laying the eggs, from twenty to forty, so that they are well covered. She sits on the nest for most of the time until the eggs hatch, never leaving them for long. The male stays close by. This is probably the only snake in which there is a seasonal monogamous union.

Stories of the hamadryads' aggressiveness have been much exaggerated. It has the reputation of being the only snake (with the exception of the black mamba and possibly the bushmaster), that attacks man unprovoked. The myth swells until on the front cover of a boys' paper you see a grim-faced young British Teak-wallah on a motor bike speeding along a jungle track with a gigantic king cobra, almost on the tip of its tail, in hot pursuit. There doesn't, however, seem to be any doubt that *Naja hannah* will attack if interfered with.

It is quite fearless; Ditmars describes it as having a 'dangerous insolence'. He also inclines to believe reports that in the breeding season after the early rains hamadryads assemble in small groups in suitable terrain. If disturbed they become quite savage, rear up to 4 feet or more and may move in to the attack. The male is also likely to be aggressive when doing guard duty over the nest. There is an entertaining story that illustrates the hamadryad's insolence. An Englishman motoring in Siam saw a large snake crossing the road. He trod on the gas but only ran over the snake's tail. He stopped the car to see what had happened and told his wife to put her head out and have a look round. She did so and fainted. The hamadryad was level with her face, trying to have a look in.

The venom of elapid snakes used to be classed as primarily neuro-toxic, and that of viperines haemotoxic – this was, and still can be, a convenient distinction but recent research has shown it to be an over-simplification of the facts and it should only be used broadly. All elapid venom is swifter-acting than viperine. The hamadryad's may not be quite so lethal as that of some of the Australian elapids, but its huge glands carry a massive charge. The fangs are short; the groove in them that carries the venom is closed over. When biting the snake makes a slight chewing motion. A case is recorded of death half-an-hour after a Burmese peasant had been bitten in the thigh. Elephants working in teak plantations have been killed by bites from hama-dryads, presumably in the trunk though it is said that hamadryads are so bright that they can pick on the one spot in an elephant's foot, at the base of the nail, where the skin is tender. One elephant died three hours after being bitten.

The common Asiatic cobra, *Naja naja*, is much smaller than *N. hannah*. From 4 to 5 feet is the average for an adult; one over 6 feet is reckoned to be large. The colour is light to dark brown with whitish rings. The hood has a spectacle mark on it; according to legend this is a mark of distinction conferred by Brahma on an ancestral cobra that had spread her hood over his face to shield it from the sun as he lay sleeping. The common cobra eats small mammals and birds and, being particularly fond of rats, it often comes close to villages and bungalows. It is found in a variety of country – brush, jungle and plain. Judging by its rat-eating, its eye-

Indian cobra *(Naja naja)*

sight seems to be well adjusted for the evening light. Its bite is
dangerous, said to cause death in 10 per cent of cases. It does not
rear very high off the ground and when it does its strike is rather
slow, though it can jink sideways like a flash when chasing a rat. Its
temperament is very different from that of *N. hannah*; no dangerous
insolence here. Individual dispositions vary from the nervous and
fidgety to the relatively docile; it can be tamed; this is an intelligent
snake though not a brilliant one. The common cobra inhabits a wide
range of India and South-east Asia. Some of the eastern varieties can
spit venom but seldom do so. *Naja celebensis*, in the Celebes, is given
a species to itself.

There are eight distinct species of African cobra. The commonest is
Naja haje, the Egyptian cobra (being sometimes known as the asp it
competes with the viper for Cleopatra's bosom).[1] This is a big dark-
coloured snake growing up to 8 feet and more. Its hood, like that of
most of the African cobras, is much narrower than that of *Naja naja*.

[1] I have remarked elsewhere on Shakespeare's herpetology. Plutarch is also
partly responsible for the confusion here. A woman of Cleopatra's intelligence is
unlikely, if she was properly informed, to have chosen *Cerastes cornutus*, the
horned viper whose bite would be more painful and probably not so lethal. On the
other hand *Naja haje* is rather large to be called a worm and secreted in a basket
of figs. However, the odds would seem to be in favour of *Naja haje*, which also
appears to have been the serpent featured in ancient Egyptian headdresses.

It likes desert country and sometimes strays across the border into Asia. In Africa it is found from Egypt to Morocco and south as far as Zambia and South-west Africa. It eats a varied diet of small desert-living animals, including jerboas and lizards. Its venom is quite powerful, but it doesn't do much harm.

Another African species is the black-lipped cobra (*Naja melano-leuca*), sometimes called the black and white cobra. It has much the same distribution south of the Sahara as *N. haje* but with a preference for forest areas. It is rather timid and goes to ground in hollow trees and termites' nests.

The black-necked Cobra (*N. nigricollis*) is smaller than *N. melano-leuca* and there are contradictory reports of its temperament, for though it can spit its venom it also sometimes shams dead. The champion venom-spitter is the ringhals or spitting cobra (*Hemachatus hemachatus*) of South and Central Africa. It ejects its venom through the fangs, which have a special cut-out at the exit of the poison canal, by muscular pressure, to a distance of 12 feet. When it spits it rears up and leans back a little and seems to be aiming intentionally at the eyes. If it scores a hit the pain and inflammation can be hideous; in very severe cases it may cause total blindness. Presumably venom-spitting is a defensive measure only to be used in emergencies. It is not efficient for catching small mammals and uses up a lot of venom. (Incidentally the Chinese variety of the common cobra has spitting powers but refuses to use them on a mongoose.) It is suggested that venom-spitting might have been developed as a defence against being trodden on by large hooved animals, but if so why have not all cobras, in suitable areas, become spitters?

Other African cobra species are two more aquatically inclined forms, the ringed water cobra (*Boulengerina annulata*) and Christy's water cobra (*Boulengerina christyi*).

We must go back to India and South-east Asia for another group of elapids, the kraits. These are moderately sized snakes with smooth scales and triangular bodies. Kipling in *Riki-tiki-tavi* committed another of his herpetological howlers by describing the krait as a minute snake lying in wait for people in the dust. There are several species of krait and some of them quite large. The banded krait (*Bungarus fasciatus*) is a handsome brown snake with white bands, maximum length 6 feet. The common or blue krait (*Bungarus caeruleus*) is a little shorter. Both these are snake-eaters. There are some smaller species. Their venom is potent. Kraits seldom bite humans. There is a sad story of two little boys who caught a small krait, tied it to a stick and brought it home. They were punished for playing with a snake. The krait, which had never raised a fang against its tormentors, was liquidated.

Back to Africa, Central, East and South, for the mambas, mainly the green (*Dendroaspis viridis*) and the black (*Dendroaspis polylepis*). These two are among the most venomous of all the *Elapidae*. The green mamba is one of the most beautiful snakes in the world. Its green is indescribable; it combines with the texture of its scales and its long head and beautifully slender tree-climber's body to give you a feeling of mystical exhilaration, something like that experienced by the author of the Book of Revelation when conjuring up his visions of that elaborately bejewelled City of God. The eyes are dark, large but well proportioned, not unduly large like those of the boomslange.

The green mamba is shorter than the black and seldom if ever exceeds 7 feet. It is also more arboreal and climbs high trees as well as bushes. It is a wonderful sight to see when it extends 2 or 3 feet of its body, horizontally, in the air to reach a further branch with its head. Margaret Lane, in her *Life with Ionides*, gives an excellent description of catching mambas. It includes an account of a green mamba striking at a bird 'while it was yet in the air'. The snake was disturbed by one of Ionides' African assistants; it began to climb and dropped the bird, an African starling. It fell 'with a tiny thud at my feet . . . its eyes open, its body still pliant and warm with the movement of life. But it was quite dead, without any visible mark. . . .'

The mamba's diet, besides birds, includes lizards and small mammals. It has well-developed teeth for seizing and masticating prey. The fangs are rather large for an elapid and placed forward under the snout. Mambas are exceptionally active snakes and can move very fast. They seem to be able almost to project themselves like green arrows. They are egg-layers; the males have been seen engaged in ritual fighting in the breeding season. Mating may take place high up in the tree tops. For all its darting activity this is a shy

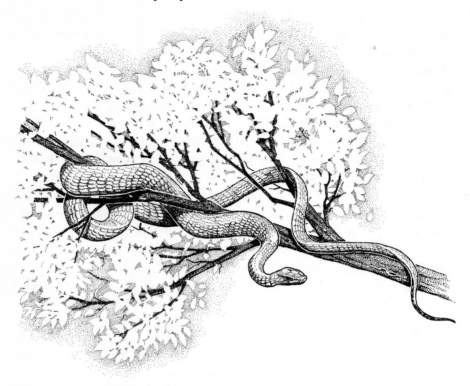

Green mamba *(Dendroaspis viridis)*

snake. Its reaction to man is to take to flight. In captivity it becomes quite quiet and had been known to take dead mice when they were offered to it on the end of a bamboo pole; but after a time it goes off its food and dies.

The black mamba is a good deal larger. The record is 14 feet. It is found over a wide area south of the Sahara. The young are green, which leads to some confusion, and turn very dark brown but never jet black as they grow up. The black mamba is also an expert climber, but it prefers bush country to forest. Its feeding habits are much the same as those of the green. Its temperament is very different. It is almost certainly the most aggressive of living venomous snakes. When startled it stays its ground and gapes its mouth wide open as if to show its fangs, and raises its head high. Perhaps its ferocity has been exaggerated; certainly it has given rise to some ripe mamba myths, like the snake overtaking a man on a galloping horse. (The recorded speed of an irritated mamba at large is a little over seven miles per hour on the flat.) But the fact remains that the black mamba can be a menace. Stories of entire African families bitten in lightning succession by disturbed mambas seem to be authentic. John Crompton, an old East African hand, tells several mamba stories in his anecdoteful little book *Snakes*. One is of a farmer ploughing with a team of six oxen. They disturbed a black mamba. It climbed up the leg of one ox, slithered over the backs of the whole team and bit four of them; two died.

Another story is about a fatal practical joke; this one is taken from a South African newspaper. A farmer – he must have been of very doubtful mentality – shot a female mamba during the breeding season. He and a chum carried it home and arranged it on the floor of the bedroom. When his wife went into the bedroom they sat back merrily waiting for the shriek. They went to the bedroom, found the door jammed and burst it open. Inside was the wife, dead, one mamba dead, and a second mamba very much alive. It had climbed into the room following the scent of the dead female. The woman, in panic, had backed and somehow managed to jam the door. A happier mamba story was told me by the late C. F. Ionides. He was sitting one night in an alfresco earth-closet with his trousers down doing his business by the light of a hurricane lamp when he felt a snake crawling over his knee. The snake crawled over him and away. It was a large black mamba. Ionides sat still as a stone. 'The sensation,' he said to me, 'now that I come to think of it, was really not at all unpleasant.'

There are other species to which I can give only a passing mention: Jameson's mamba (*D. jamesonii*), smaller than the black mamba, found in the rain forests and lake regions of Central Africa, can be either green or brown with sometimes a black and green tail. The West African mamba (*D. viridis*) is green with dark-edged scales, and in the Transvaal there is *Dendroaspis* mamba, but whether this is a separate species or merely a variation of the black mamba is uncertain; the modern tendency is to regard it as a variation.

Now for Australia, where the great majority of the snakes are elapid, sixty species in all, some of them small and relatively inoffensive but several of them large and very dangerous indeed. Perhaps this is why the Australians, judging by those I have met, tend to be a nation of ophidophobes. I once stayed a weekend in the Paris flat of an old Australian friend, Sam White, the *Evening Standard* Paris correpondent, the least neurotic of men. I had with me in my pocket an Aesculapian snake which I had caught in the forest of Fontainebleau. Sam's reaction when he found me giving it a swim in his bath was alarmingly intense. He controlled himself magnificently but made me promise to keep Aesculapius locked up in a suitcase. I think his fear was a rational product of childhood in a land of dangerous snakes. He certainly has never seemed to be suffering from the castration anxiety which the Freudians will, inevitably, tell you is at the root of snake-terror.

Deadliest of the Australian elapids is the taipan (*Oxyuranus scutellatus*), inhabiting parts of eastern Australia and especially the Cape York Peninsula. This reaches a length of 11 feet, has fangs half an inch long and enormous poison glands carrying twice as much venom as any other Australian species. It is an elongated brown snake with a triangular body rather like a krait's. It is ferocious in the extreme and will attack on sight, coiling, waving its tail and biting quickly several times. Mercifully it is rare and lives away from the haunts of men. It has bitten only a few people, but every one of those died, and a horse bitten by a taipan died in five minutes.

Much commoner and highly dangerous though not quite so lethal is the tiger snake (*Notechis scutatus*), abundant in eastern and South Australia and even found in Tasmania. It averages 5 feet with a maximum of 7 feet. The most usual colour is brown with yellowish stripes; there may be a good deal of variation, from orange to black. The body is rather thick. Though essentially a ground snake it climbs bushes. It is viviparous, or rather ovoviparous, like most Australian elapids and produces vast litters of fifty to sixty, the record being seventy-two. Its venom is even more potent than that of the taipan, super-elapid venom which acts quickly, paralysing the respiratory centres. It causes more deaths than all the other Australian snakes together. It is bad-tempered and bites with a fast strike that makes it look almost as if it were jumping.

Acanthopis antarticus is commonly known as the death adder. This is a misnomer but an understandable one, because although it is an elapid it has a deceptively viperine appearance with a thick body and broad head. Its venom is not so powerful as the tiger snake's, but quite powerful enough to be dangerous. It has large fangs and bites deep. It is quite small, only 2 feet long, reddish-brown with dark bands; its scales are keeled and it has a spine on its tail. It lives on dry sandy soil which its camouflage neatly matches. It can all too easily be trodden on. It is distributed over much of the dry country of Australia, except for Victoria, and also turns up in New Guinea and the Moluccas.

Those are the most dangerous species. The brown snake (*Demamsia textilis*) is another large elapid with a fierce disposition; this is the only one that is truly oviparous. The black snake (*Pseudechis porphyriacus*) is a 6-footer which spreads its neck like a miniature cobra hood. The males are remarkable for their territorial battles which have been described by David Fleay, Director of the Fauna Reserve at West Burleigh, Queensland. These are more strenuous than most snakes' wrestling matches. The adversaries twine round each other, rolling over and over, with regular intervals in between bouts like human boxers. They go on until they are exhausted. The Australian copperhead (*Denisonia superba*), not to be confused with the North American viperine copperhead, is a 5-foot snake which lives in south-eastern Australia and Tasmania. (Note the hardiness of these antipodean elapids; it makes one feel we British are lucky not to have tiger snakes in the Isle of Wight.) It is venomous enough, but very shy.

There are several smaller Australian elapids whose venom is weak; this, says K. P. Schmidt, 'might be derived secondarily with decrease of size and change of food habits, these snakes being mainly insect-eaters. A typical example is the bandy-bandy (*Vermicella annulata*), a small, dark brown and white snake that looks like a burrower but isn't. Its bite is not much worse than a bee's sting.'

The American elapids are the coral snakes, distributed through the southern USA down to northern Argentina and Peru. There are some forty or more in the genus *Micurus*. They are small, very pretty snakes with brightly coloured bands of red, black, blue, yellow. The Arizona coral snake (*Micrurus euryxanthus*) is a bold red, white and blue. The eastern coral snake (*M. fulvius*) has a striking alternation of brownish-pink and narrower yellow bands. Coral snakes are certainly secretive and it is a little odd that they should be so brightly coloured. They eat lizards and small snakes. Several species wriggle the tips of their tails in the air as if they were heads. Their fangs are small; they are docile and rarely attempt to bite when handled, but their venom is extremely powerful and has caused the death of many an incautious hominid.

There are several nonvenomous colubrines that look very like coral snakes, especially the milk snake (*Lampropeltis doliata*), first cousin to the king snake. I remember how I used when a small boy to read over and over again a fatally misleading passage about coral snakes in the volume on reptiles in the Rev. J. G. Wood's *Natural History*, which was then my bible. After rhapsodising over the beauty of the coral snake Wood went on about its gentle disposition. It was, he admitted, possible that it might be venomous, but even if it was it was only very mildly so and could be regarded as virtually harmless. I yearned to possess one. I wonder if any lives were lost by this well-meaning (unless the Rev. J. G. was a crypto-diabolist) passage. Incidentally, the shape of these pretty snakes, though slender and tapering, is somehow not quite satisfactory; they look faintly like toys.

The precise relationship of the sea snake family, the *Hydrophiidae*, to the land-living elapids is uncertain. They are thought to be closest to the cobras. They are a most fascinating family. Most of them are completely adapted to marine life and never come ashore. Their bodies are flattened from side to side and their tails are so compressed that the tips are like the blades of oars. They move through water with perfect ease. Nobody seems to have measured the speed with which they swim, but it must be on a par with that of fishes. The nostrils, set high, have special valves to keep the water out. The scales are smooth; most species have lost the large overlapping ventral scales that help other snakes to get a purchase on land surfaces.

How far they go out to sea varies a lot. One genus, *Laticauda*, has remained amphibious. It has kept its ventral scales and when it comes ashore to lay its eggs it gets about quite easily. This is the only egg-laying species. The others are all viviparous – an obvious advantage for an air-breathing animal that is spending its entire life at sea. In Lake Taal, in Luzon in the Philippines, there is one species, *Hydrophis semperi*, a close relation of the blue banded sea snake, *H. cyanocinctus*, that appears to be permanently landlocked.

The distribution of sea snakes is fairly wide but specialised. You find them in warm tropical seas near the Asian coasts, from the Persian Gulf all the way to Japan and Australia. The black and yellow sea snake (*Pelamis platurus*), which is probably the widest-ranging species, has crossed the Pacific and is found on the northern coast of South America. This is a handsome little 3-foot snake with a long head.

The fangs of sea snakes are shorter than those of cobras and the canal for conducting the venom is a groove on the outside of the tooth. The venom is very powerful and on eels it produces almost instantaneous paralysis; there are probably variations in the venom-potency of different species. The effects on man are rather curious; in some cases there is no pain at the site of the bite but severe muscular pain may come on later. The kidneys are affected and the urine turns reddish-brown.

Reports about the temperaments of sea snakes out of water are varying. Some say they are quite docile and seldom bite fishermen when they disentangle them from their nets. Others tell you they snap viciously. A naval rating whose ship was anchored off the Pacific side of the Isthmus of Panama decided to swim ashore; he found himself in the middle of a shoal of sea snakes, but none attempted to do him harm.

There are some specialised forms such as *Microcephalophis gracilis* with a slender neck and head and a grossly thickened body. It is an insatiable eel-eater. Schmidt suggests that this peculiar shape may have its advantages; the thick abdomen serves as a base or fulcrum from which the strike at prey is launched. He compares it to the extinct pleiosaurus.

The largest known sea snakes are members of the *Hydrophis* sub-family. They have not so far been found to be more than 8 feet long, though mythomaniacs and sensationalists go on hoping, and the best of serpentine luck to them. Sea snakes like to bask on the surface of the water or lie in wait for fish, which instinctively congregate near floating objects. They have often been seen in literally thousands. The most sensational account, often quoted though one cannot help doubting whether it is ever fully believed, is given by a Mr Lowe. In 1932, from a ship near the Strait of Malacca, he saw 'a solid mass of sea snakes twisted thickly together' in a band which he estimated was 10 feet wide and extended for 60 miles! The species was *Astrotia stokesi*, about 5 ft long, brightly coloured red and black.

In Japan sea snakes are a great delicacy and there is a big trade in them. They are spitted on a bamboo and roasted or smoked. The *Laticaudae* used, at any rate before the war, to be the favourite species. They would collect in great swarms in caves on some of the Philippine Islands.

Chapter 9

Venomous Snakes

The *Viperidae*: vipers and pit-vipers

In some ways the *Viperidae* represent the last word in the evolution of poisonous snakes. Their fangs are large and hollow and extremely efficient; they are not mere fixtures in the jaw but can be erected for action and folded back afterwards. The venom glands are large and secrete a bigger dose than most of the elapids, though the venom itself is not quite so potent.[1] There is a tendency among many species of vipers to be bloated and sluggish; but we must not let this warp our judgement. The *Viperidae* may not be a family of all-round athletes like the *Elapidae*; yet they include many alarmingly active members, especially in the New World.

We have touched on some of the vipers of the Old World in the chapter on Evolution and Classification, and will come to the single British example in the next chapter. Only a few of the *Viperinae* – the true vipers – have travelled outside Africa. Among them are the beautiful Russell's viper (*Vipera russelli*) or tic polonga (see p. 158) of India; also the handsome Palestinian viper, quite large and distinctly dangerous. The saw-scaled viper (*Echis carinatus*) is found in India and Ceylon and Africa. This small snake is beautifully marked with pastel shades of greyish-pink and pinkish-grey on a brown background and blends well with its dry surroundings. It is extremely venomous. When angry or frightened it coils round and round in figures of eight, rubbing its scales together to make a noise like a kettle boiling. Another interesting little African genus is *Causus*, the night adders. These inhabit Central and East-Central Africa. They are small and slender and not at all characteristically viperine in appear-

[1] It has been calculated that if one of the big viperids such as a gaboon viper or a diamond-backed rattlesnake could be stocked up with the venom of the tiger snake (see p. 90) it would have enough to kill 400 men.

ance; the scales on their heads show affinities with the colubrids, which suggests to the comparative anatomist that they may be primitive viper-types; they are also egg-layers. They have long venom glands that go some way back into the body. There are four species, among them the pleasingly named green night adder (*C. resimus*). The venom is not very potent to judge – a rather dangerous thing to do, perhaps – by Ionides, who treated a night adder's bite lightly.

The African desert vipers include our old friend *Cerastes cornutus*,[1] the horned viper of North Africa, very short – 2 feet long – thickish, with its curiously bulbous head; it is a good deal more venomous than the common viper. *Cerastes* can move by sidewinding and likes to lie buried in the sand. So does another desert species known as the dwarf viper. Another African group is the burrowing *Atractaspis* genus, the mole vipers. These, like the night adders, have slight colubrid affinities and lay eggs. The head is narrow but the fangs are almost too big for the mouth. Least known of vipers is Fea's viper, *Azemiops feae*, with colubrid affinities in its scalation more marked than those of the night adder. It is a beautiful snake, with a yellow head and banded body. Its fangs are very short. It is found in Burma, Indo-China and China (Japan is viper-free).

The African genus *Atheris* is unique in being a group of arboreal tree vipers;[2] small and leaf-green, they are viperine in form but have prehensile tails and keeled scales.

I have left until last the great genus *Bitis*. Its chief members are the puff-adder, the gaboon viper and the rhinoceros viper. They are, in spite of anything you may hear to the contrary, some of the most beautiful snakes in the world. The puff adder (*Bitis arietans*) is the commonest, distributed all over the open country of Africa from the

---

[1] There are also the two false *Cerastes* of Persia and Palestine. *Pseudo cerastes fieldi*, the Palestinian species, was discovered in 1930. Both have valves in their nostrils to keep the sand out. A somewhat mysterious little viper known only in part of Baluchistan combines the features of desert vipers with keeled scales that are ordinarily associated with arboreal snakes; it has a pair of wing-like scales on its snout.

[2] There may be some slight confusion here with the arboreal pit-vipers such as Trimeresurus.

southern border of the Sahara to the Cape; it also turns up in Morocco and Arabia. It is very thick in the body with a big head and grows to a length of 5 feet. Because of its rather grotesque proportions it is sometimes misdescribed as bloated and hideous. The pattern of its body colour is very subtle, varying from light brown to grey with broken semi-circular yellowish markings cross-wise. It blends wonderfully well with sand and dust. The puff adder in spite of its bulk is agile, so agile that it is sometimes credited with mythical athletic feats like jumping backwards. Its favourite diet consists of small mammals, mostly rodents. It strikes very quickly; sometimes it waits before going after the dying prey which it tracks down with its tongue in collaboration with Jacobson's organ. It has been known to use its fangs as hooks to hook the prey into its mouth. The venom is powerfully haemotoxic and can be fatal. The hiss is particularly noisy and accompanied by impressive inflation of the throat. (See p. 156 for a 'tame' puff adder: Ionides again.) It is ovoviparous and, as if aware of its unpopularity, produces broods of seventy. There are some smaller species in South Africa which are sidewinders and can climb a bit.

Gaboon viper *(Bitis gabonica)*

The gaboon viper is even thicker in the body and bigger in the head than the puff-adder. It grows to a length of 5 feet and 6 feet has been recorded. Its fangs are over 1½ inches long and its venom glands truly enormous. The venom is more potent than the puff adder's. A full shot from both fangs would be likely to kill a man. R. Martin Perkins, Curator of the St Louis Reptile House, was struck in the left forefinger by one fang of a specimen which he and an assistant were treating for parasites. He was in hospital for three weeks. During the first few hours he lost consciousness and they thought he was going to die; he probably would have done if he had not been given blood transfusions and antivenene injections.

The markings of the gaboon viper are lovely. Variations of purple, brown and pink – never glaring, almost pastel shades – are arranged in geometrical patterns that have for me a strong African association. The head is light beige with dark triangles on the cheeks. The eye is silver. Ditmars, generally most appreciative of the beauty of serpents, ran amok when describing *Bitis gabonica*. 'Upon this awesome form', he wrote, 'the symmetrical patterns and really beautiful hues repel, rather than soften the picture. The design looks more like a pattern in bizarre weaving than markings of a serpent.' Strange. On me, at any rate, the effect is exactly the opposite. The pattern is marvellously attractive. I wonder textile designers don't try to copy it.

The gaboon viper's distribution is narrower than the puff-adder's. It inhabits the tropical rain forest belt from West to East Africa. It is quite common in its proper habitat. Ionides' house on its Tanzanian plateau nearly always held a few specimens. It feeds mainly by night on small mammals. It strikes fast, sinks its fangs in deep and often holds on until the prey dies between its jaws.

This huge viper's docility, by day anyway, is extraordinary. It never seems to attack man. Some Africans are far less frightened of it than of the harmless little geckoes which have become objects of superstition. A small native boy has been known to arrive at a zoologist's camp dragging on a string a large live gaboon viper to sell.

The third of the three great *Bitis* species, the rhinoceros viper (*Bitis nasicornis*), has much the same distribution as the gaboon viper, though it is a good deal less common and more likely to be found near water and in West rather than East Africa. It is shorter, 4 feet being the maximum, and its head is smaller. The horns on its snout are quite noticeable. Its skin is quite exquisite, more beautiful than any Oriental rug. The top of its head is blue with a black arrow pointing forward. The back carries a row of broken pale blue oblongs with yellow lines through them. The sides have crimson-lake triangles marked with blue borders. The groundwork is beige. Though the colours are brighter than those of *B. gabonica* the design is more complex, with an association of Islamic rather than pagan African art. Both skins despite their arresting patterns probably have survival value as camouflage rather than as warnings.

Now for the pit vipers, the family *Crotalidae*, the great majority of which are found in the New World. The pits in the head have already been mentioned. They are especially well developed in the subfamily *Crotalinae*, the rattlesnakes. The pit is a complex organ; it is enclosed by a hollow in the maxillary bone of the upper jaw. It has an outer and inner chamber separated by a membrane of skin and connective tissue with nerve-endings. The inner chamber connects with the outside by a tiny pore opening just in front of the eye. This organ exists, though in a very simplified form, in some pythons and boas. For a long time its purpose was a mystery, though the German herpetologist Franz Leidig suggested a century ago that it was a sense organ. Then, in the 1930s experiments by Noble and Schmidt showed that the pits responded to small variations of temperature and infra-red rays. The degree of sensitivity is very precise. The idea is that snakes with pits can locate warm-blooded and perhaps also cold-blooded animals that pass close by as they lie in wait. The evolution of pits and why they are found in some species and not others is still a mystery. The pit sorts out the *Crotalidae* from the other vipers. The crotalins are distinguished by the rattle. There is something disturbing about this organ; it spoils the symmetry of otherwise beautiful snakes that ought, one feels, to end in pointed tails. These faintly comical caudal accessories are in dubious taste. None the less they are fascinating. The rattle is made up of interlocking horny segments that take the place of the conical scale which covers the tip of the tail in other snakes. Each segment consists of three lobes. The infant rattlesnake at birth has no rattle, only a horny knob. The first rattle-segment is formed when it sheds its skin for the first time. After that

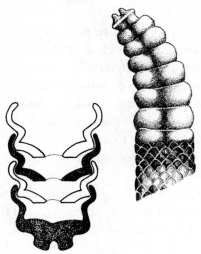

Rattlesnake's rattle with diagram
showing interlocking tail segments
which make the noise

a new segment is grown with every shedding of the skin, which happens about four or more times a year. But you can't tell the age of a rattlesnake by counting the segments and dividing by four because in the stress of wild life they often get broken off. Eight is an average and a rattle with eight segments is usually carried off the ground in a semi-erect position. In the peaceful club life of captivity the record number of segments is twenty-nine.

The rattle sound is a dry whirring and the rattle vibrates so fast that it looks blurred. It can be kept up for quite a long time, many minutes, and it carries up to thirty yards. Captive snakes rattle less readily than wild ones. The most rational assumption is that rattling warns intruders to keep their distance. It is an arresting sound. If the rattle doesn't work and the intruder comes closer the snake coils and rears up in an aggressive posture ready to strike, puffs out its body and hisses furiously. The survival value of a rattle in a country where hooved animals may be charging around can be considerable. And there were far more of these ungulates at large in prehistoric America when rattles were evolved than during the nineteenth century when the Wild West was opened up.

There are various other theories about possible alternative uses of the rattle. Some suggest it is a signal to other rattlesnakes for help! Others suggest it might be a means of attracting prey. The first two used to be dismissed because it was thought that snakes were stone deaf, but this is not so: some can respond to low notes within the compass of a rattlesnake's rattle. Of the third suggestion it may be noted that several species of snake do use their tails to attract prey, especially prey such as the observant and curious-seeming lizard.

There are twenty-eight known species of rattlesnake, divided into two genera: *Crotalus* and *Sistrurus*. Rattlesnakes are found in southern Canada, North America, South America east of the Andes down to northern Argentina. Some say their original home is northern Mexico, Texas and Arizona. The nearer to the Equator the higher up do you find the rattlesnake. Most prefer dry ground and bush country. There are a few which take to forest and even swamp, and do a little climbing and swimming.

The largest rattlesnakes are the diamond-back species, *Crotalus adamanteus* and *Crotalus atrox*. *C. adamanteus*, sometimes known as the eastern diamond-back, inhabits Florida and regions east to Louisiana, never being found more than 100 miles from the coast. It averages 5 to 6 feet, but 9 feet has been recorded. It eats rabbits and birds. It is aggressive when approached. Like all rattlesnakes it gapes its mouth wide open with its jaws at an angle of nearly 180° when it strikes.

C. atrox, the western diamond-back, is slightly smaller, likes dry and semi-desert country from Missouri to Texas and California and north-eastern Mexico. Its cousin, *C. horridus*, the timber rattlesnake, also known as the banded one, is found in the eastern United States. It is large, up to 6 feet. This was the first rattlesnake to be met with by the early colonists, who sent home sensational reports of its size and ferocity. It is the commonest rattlesnake in the USA. The prairie rattlesnake (*C. viridis*) inhabits the western areas of the USA. Its average length is 3 feet, maximum 5 feet. These two species between them are found in a large number of states, always excepting Maine, Michigan and Minnesota.

Crotalus devissus, the tropical rattlesnake or cascabel, which is Spanish for rattle, inhabits most of Central and South America. It is nearly as large as the diamond-backs, with an even more savage disposition. Its venom is very powerful and contains both neurotoxic and haemotoxic elements. It has a peculiar effect on the neck muscles, which accounts for the superstition that the cascabel breaks the neck when it bites. There is a western Mexican species, *Crotalus basilicus*, whose venom has the same properties.

An interesting desert-dwelling species is *Crotalus cerastes*, the sidewinder, a small snake with little scaly horns over its eyes. This is the only rattlesnake to move by sidewinding.

Of the *Sistrurus* genus, the pigmy rattlesnakes (the Indian name is *Massasagua*), one member, *S. miliarus*, inhabits the south-eastern United States. This is a pretty little rattler, less than 2 feet long, greenish-grey with black and reddish-brown blotches. Another slightly larger species is found in Indiana, Illinois, Michigan and Wisconsin and as far east as the Finger Lakes region of New York State. It has been encountered, heaven help it, in the suburbs of Chicago. There is another pygmy species in Mexico. These pygmy rattlesnakes, like the African night vipers, have colubrid affinities. They are not thought to be very dangerous but can inflict a nasty bite. W. T. Davies, an entomologist, was bitten by a 9-inch specimen in North Carolina. He mistook it for a young hog-nosed snake. Within forty-eight hours his arm was black and blue and his left side swelled up. One can imagine, as Schmidt says, the catastrophic effect of a bite from one of the larger, more dangerous, species. The pygmy's rattle is very short, as one might expect in a primitive genus.

That is a fairly representative selection, if a much abridged one. There are at least eighteen species of true *Crotalus* in Mexico alone, half of them very small. (One, Stejneger's rattlesnake, has a very long tail with a tiny rattle.) There is a great deal of variation in colour with several black forms, and in Arizona one pink one – *C. nuntius*.

Temperaments also vary. Some of the diamond-backs do very well in captivity. And *Crotalus ruber*, a particularly handsome south-western Californian species or subspecies, has been induced to breed in more than one zoo. At San Diego it has been crossed with other species. The young males are so much at home in their cages that they will perform their ritual wrestling matches. Ditmars bred diamond-backs (viviparous like all rattlesnakes) in the New York Zoo and seemed almost inclined to credit them with parental care. A 6-foot female from Florida gave birth to a litter of nine. Until her accouchement she had been very tame and had stopped rattling. After the birth she rattled persistently and struck savagely at her keeper whenever he opened the door of her cage to change her water. Rattlesnakes mate in much the same way as other snakes; they hold the record for copulation, lasting in one case $22\frac{3}{4}$ hours. Attempts at homosexual mating have been observed in captivity.

Another record held by rattlesnakes is for the length of time they live after being 'killed'. Klauber decapitated thirteen specimens and found that the heads were dangerous for twenty minutes to one hour after they had been severed. For up to forty minutes the heads would bite sticks and open their mouths and erect their fangs if a hand approached; their eye pupils contracted. At forty-three minutes one head bit a stick and discharged its venom. After fifty minutes there was little 'life' in the heads. The headless bodies did not attempt to strike or rattle but squirmed a lot. One body righted itself from an inverted position seven hours and forty-three minutes after decapitation. The heart went on beating and in the case of one sidewinder was still active after fifty-nine hours. British readers may have heard the country superstition that an adder goes on wriggling until sunset.

Yet another record is probably held by the timber rattlesnake, which congregates for hibernation in very large numbers. The story is told of an American settler who built himself a log cabin in winter and woke up on the first warm spring morning to find himself entirely surrounded by ranks of rattlesnakes.

Some of the uses and abuses to which men put rattlesnakes are curious. They have been employed as murder weapons in real life as well as in crime fiction. Between the wars a citizen of California tried to kill his wife by making her put her foot through a hole in an orange-crate into which he had inserted some diamond-backs. She got her divorce. They do not appear to have been used as weapons of war, as vipers were by Hannibal, who ordered his admiral to sling viper-bombs, baskets full of vipers, at the Roman fleet, thereby somewhat tarnishing his reputation as a generous opponent. But a Californian suicide broke into a cage of rattlesnakes and was not content until he had received eighty-three snake bites.

Rattlesnakes have been held in the mouths of religious fanatics of various sects from white evangelists to Hopi Indians. Belief in the magical properties of rattlesnakes' flesh and bones was so fervent among nineteenth- and early twentieth-century American hicks that snake-oil,[1] which would make you so supple you could tie yourself into a knot, was part of the travelling quack's stock in trade. One Californian factory sells several thousand cans of rattlesnakes' flesh each year. . . .

We must pass on to the non-rattling *Crotalidae*. In North America these are represented by the copperheads and the water-moccasins, both of the genus *Ancistrodon*.

The copperhead (*A. contortrix*) is a pretty little snake 2 feet 6 inches to 4 feet long, with a mottled skin the colour of autumn beech leaves. It is found in the south-eastern States. One subspecies ranges from southern New England, Pennsylvania and the Middle West; another inhabits the plains of the Atlantic coast and the Gulf of Florida; another in Texas and Kansas; and yet another, with a black belly, in southern Texas and northern Mexico. It eats caterpillars and grasshoppers as well as the inevitable small mammals. Its bite is painful but seldom fatal. When enraged it vibrates its tail against leaves, making a noise like a rattlesnake.

The water-moccasin (*A. piscivorus*) is aquatic but rather sluggish. It inhabits the swamps of Florida and Mississippi. It is black or dark brown; the young are lighter with bright yellow tails. It feeds on fish and frogs and mammals and birds. The maximum length is 5 feet. It has a rather sinister appearance with a thick viperine body and gapes its white mouth wide open with fangs erect when disturbed. Hence the Negro name for it, the cotton-mouth. Its venom is potent. There is a Mexican species (*A. bilineatus*) which is more colourful. It does surprisingly well in captivity, breeding, and living for twenty years.

There are several species of ancystrodon in the Old World. One, *A. halys*, ranges from south-eastern Russia via Central Asia to Japan where the subspecies is called *Ancistrodon halys blomhoffi*. There is

---

[1] The Chinese sell a liqueur called snake-wine. It is exceedingly powerful and makes green Chartreuse seem like lime juice. The only time I drank it I felt as if the top of my skull was lifting. If it does contain any ophidian ingredient it is probably snake's gall-bladder. A tincture of this in rice wine is still taken by Chinese as a cure for rheumatism.

also a Himalayan species, and a quite distinct Malayan species that lays eggs.

And now for the genus *Bothrops*. There could be confusion here because the pit vipers of the Old World were often classed under *Bothrops*. Fortunately some rationalist has come to the rescue by classing nearly all the New World species under the genus *Bothrops* and all the Old World species under the genus *Trimeresurus*; we will follow his light. I will resist the temptation to begin with the most sensational species, the dreaded *fer de lance*, and start with the palm vipers. These are tropical arboreal vipers with prehensile tails and large wide heads; they are quite small, around 3 feet. There are several species inhabiting bush and jungle country in southern Mexico, Central and South America. They have a habit of fastening their tails round a branch and hanging down and then coiling sideways in the air parallel to the ground with the head held ready to strike. This can be dangerous for any hominid blundering through the jungle as he may chance on an arboreal *Bothrops* at a level with his face. The fangs are large, the venom potent.

A typical palm viper is *Bothrops schlegeli*, or the horned palm viper, with two or three little scaly horns on his nose. Its colour may be olive green speckled with red and black or pale lemon yellow speckled with black. The expression of *B. schlegeli* can seem faintly whimsical. But it caused several deaths among a gang of workers cutting a track through the jungle in Honduras. There are several small 2-foot terrestrial species of *Bothrops* often called the hog-nosed vipers, quite dangerous. An allied species is *Bothrops mummifera*, the jumping viper! In Spanish it is called *mano de piedra* because it looks like an agricultural implement of that name. It is about 3 feet long, very thick in the body with rough scales. And it really can jump, taking off from a log and launching its body through the air for a distance of 2 or even 3 feet. Because of this startling habit and its rather sinister appearance and bad temper it used to be much dreaded, but its venom is considerably weaker than that of its relations.

The king of the *Bothrops* genus is *B. atrox*,[1] the *fer de lance*. This is a magnificent viper which grows to a length of, exceptionally, over

---

[1] It used to be called *Lachesis lanceolatus*, but the generic name *Lachesis* is now reserved for the bushmaster.

8 feet, though the average is much less. It is strong, quite slender with a characteristic lance-shaped head. Colour varies from olive to reddish-brown with dark crossbands, light-edged triangular cross-bands and a yellowish chin and throat which accounts for its Spanish name of *Barba Amarilla*. It inhabits southern Mexico, Central and South America and used to be all too plentiful in some Caribbean islands. Viviparous, it produces huge litters of sixty to seventy. The young are a foot long when born, fully fanged and very dangerous. It is a quick-moving, savage snake with large fangs and big poison glands. The potency of its venom is illustrated by a well-known story from the Serum Station at Tela, Honduras. An Indian railway worker was bitten by a *fer de lance* and brought home. His wife had rasped her finger with a nutmeg-grater. She bathed the fang punctures on her husband's leg. The husband died in two hours. The wife died the next morning from the venom she had absorbed through her sore finger-tip.[1] The symptoms of a *fer de lance* bite include internal bleeding and alarming discoloration in the area of the bite due to the effect on the capillaries.

Rats form the *fer de lance's* favourite diet and though it is originally a bush- and forest-dweller it will come near human habitations such as cane cutters' huts. It caused several deaths during the digging of the Panama Canal. In the West Indies it used to be particularly common in the island of Martinique. There are terrifying legends[2] of swarms of *fers de lance* fleeing from the eruption of Mont Pelé in 1905 and biting everyone in their path.

In Jamaica the *fer de lance* was such a menace to sugar cane cutters that the mongoose was imported from India to deal with them. This measure was not a total success. The little mammalian *conquistadores*

[1] The record story of this type of accident comes from Rhodesia. It is said that a man wearing leather gaiters was bitten by a black mamba. The mamba's fangs, being short, failed to pierce the man's skin, though they did penetrate the gaiters, discharging venom. Twenty years later the man's son put on his father's old shooting gaiters. He had a scratch on his calf. He died. This story was hold me by my friend James Stern.

[2] The legend, something in it somewhere, *au fond*, I suppose, of snakes retreating from a catastrophe is quite widespread. As a boy in Devonshire I was told by an imaginative friend about swarms of adders marching on Budleigh Salterton after a fire on Woodbury Common.

(celebrated in the calypso 'Sly Mongoose, de name gone abroad') did liquidate a certain number of *fers de lance*, but they also wiped out most of the nonvenomous snakes and then took to killing chickens. However, by now the *fer de lance* has been almost, if not completely, exterminated in Jamaica.

There are several closely allied species or subspecies in Brazil, popularly known as *jararacas*. The commonest of these, both rather smaller than *B. atrox*, are Maximilian's viper (*B. neuwidei*) and *B. jaracussu*, thicker in the body with a larger head. There is also a unique arboreal species, the island viper, *B. insularis*, 3 to 4 feet long, pale brown with darker brown crossbars, which lords it over the tiny island of Quermada Grande near the Bay of Santos. It preys on birds, with which the island abounds, as it is a resting place for migrants. The venom of *B. insularis*, like that of all bird-eating snakes, is potent and very fast-acting.

The largest and most venomous of all the South American snakes is the poetically named *Lachesis mutus* – Silent Fate – commonly known as the bushmaster. (It used to be classed as a *Bothrops* and was considered a close relation of *B. atrox*, but is now given a genus to itself.) This is a superb snake, slender and athletic. Its length ranges from 9 to 12 feet and there used to be reports or rumours of giant 14-footers. The ground colour is light brown, sometimes with a pinkish tinge, and large dark triangular patches. This is the only ovoviparous crotalid. It inhabits Costa Rica, Central America and, at one time anyway, Trinidad. It has huge inch-long fangs and its venom is more potent than that of the *fer de lance*. It has a most aggressive temperament and will take the offensive if approached, coiling sideways into a striking position. Its tail vibrates and makes a noise like a rattle. Bushmasters in captivity almost invariably refuse to feed and they have never, so far as is known, been tamed. There are plenty of myths about them chasing men for long distances, none of them authenticated.

Back to the Old World for that interesting genus of pit-vipers, *Trimeresurus*. It can be conveniently divided into two groups, arboreal with prehensile tails, and terrestrial without them. The arboreal *Trimeresuri* are green or brown, the terrestrial are brown or multi-coloured. They are all small, but the ground snakes are rather larger.

The longest of the arboreals is *Trimeresurus cantori*, record length 3 feet 9 inches, found in the Nicobar Islands, green with a yellow or white line along each side. *T. puniceus* of Borneo is brown but has a red tail, an unassuming snake that never climbs more than a few feet above ground level. The well-known temple viper (*T. wagleri*) is most vividly coloured in youth: bright green with a row of red and white spots along the back. The adults are darker, almost black on the back with green and yellow crossbars. In the wild state it seems to be nearly as gentle and languid – except when feeding – as it becomes in the Snake Temple at Penang. Its venom is not potent.

The largest of the terrestrial *Trimeresuri* is *T. flavoridis*, the habu, which has a thickish body and reaches a length of 5 feet; it is dangerously venomous and was dreaded by American troops on Okinawa Island during World War Two. Another curious ground species is Jerdon's mountain viper, *T. jerdoni*, dark green with black markings, found in Tibet, western China and Burma.

Chapter 10

British Snakes at Home – and Some Close European Relatives

Two colubrines and one viper. The grass snake and the smooth snake; and the 'adder'. They are all we have, and we must make the most of them. The smooth snake is now very rare. The grass snake is not quite so common as it was and dealers are now selling them at £1·75 each. And every day with more and more motoring and the cutting down of hedgerows, the spread of towns and bungaloid growth, the terrain becomes less favourable.

The grass snake (*Natrix natrix*) is a splendid snake, admirably adapted to a damp island. Its distribution is widespread; you find it in most of Europe, parts of Asia and North Africa. There are considerable local variations, including black or melanistic ones in parts of Germany and Denmark; also quite close relations in North America and Mexico.

The English grass snake, or ringed snake, which is really a better name, is olive green along the back with a pretty collar of orange, or primrose or nearly white, behind its head. There are black spots on its sides and its belly is speckled with black or pale primrose or white with the black extending over most of the lower parts. Its throat is white or pale yellow. Its upper lip is white or yellow and the sutures between the shields are black. Malcolm Smith records two individuals with a distinct tinge of blue on their upper parts.

Complete melanism has not been seen in England, but partial albinism has been recorded in several cases. One beautiful specimen lived for some months in the London Zoo. A lyrical description of it is given by the late Joan Procter in a Note in *Proceedings of the Zoological Society*, London, 1926. Its ground colour was ivory white, creamy on top of the head and the collar was also cream coloured. On the parts of its body which are normally black the skin was translucent and the flesh – pale mauve with a pink tinge – could be seen through it. The iris of the eye was pale orange, the pupil dark red. The base of the tongue was pink and the tip ivory-white. 'The general effect was that of a very pale and fragile creature carved in ivory with jewels for eyes.'

This is a shapely snake, slender but not attenuated. It has a quite long tail. Its scales are keeled. Its favourite food is the frog, which it seizes, often by a hindleg, and proceeds to swallow. The last stage, when the face of the frog is entirely surrounded by the distorted head of the grass snake, is a rather terrible sight. The frog, says Malcolm Smith, may utter plaintive cries even when it is in the gullet. Many a frog has been saved by being regurgitated as a result of some sudden intrusion. *Natrix* also eats newts, but it often rejects the crested newt after seizing it. According to J. W. Steward a captive American water-snake (*Natrix sipedon fasciata*) swallowed a crested newt, regurgitated it after a few minutes, covered with thick white slime, and died within an hour.

Grass snakes have also been known to eat new-born mice, new-born birds and small birds' eggs and bumble-bees. I forcibly fed one specimen with an appetising-looking beetle, when I could not get any frogs, and it didn't seem to suffer any ill effects. I released it soon afterwards.

Colonel Wilkins of Camberley induced several of his grass snakes to eat dead mice, one of which was already beginning to decompose. When a live mouse was offered, a grass snake seized it at once but let it go the moment the mouse retaliated by biting it. (Some of the European colubrines which are no larger than the grass snake eat mice easily because they are constrictors.) The grass snake is a voracious eater. An adult may be satisfied with one or two large frogs for a few days, but Boulenger mentions twenty very small frogs being eaten at a meal and Rollinat records nine smallish gudgeon (a small freshwater fish) being swallowed in a few hours. The grass snake drinks water plentifully, and in captivity will drink milk. It often feeds early, around 7 a.m.

You seldom if ever find *Natrix* far from water. It is an excellent swimmer, and has been seen crossing the Menai Strait between Wales and Anglesey; one was caught 25 miles out to sea in the Bay of Biscay.

This is an active, athletic snake and can climb well in bushes. An ideal locale for a grass snake is a secluded hedgerow in a field near a stream or pond where there are frogs and tadpoles. Its length full-grown is seldom more than 3 feet, but the record for the United Kingdom is 5 feet 9 inches from Glamorganshire. The largest specimen I ever caught was 3 feet 1 inch, but it had lost nearly all its tail in some accident. This was in eastern Devon in the hills inland above Sidford, in a rather exposed patch of country quite high up, over 600 feet. In Sussex, near Pulborough, I saw what looked to be a truly gigantic grass snake in ideal terrain at the edge of a froggy marsh. It dashed off down an empty rabbit burrow. I went back next day and it was there again, and again it darted down the burrow. I flung myself down and reached for its tail but just missed it. As far as I could judge its body was a size larger in diameter – and not merely distended with frog – than that of any grass snake I have ever come across. As with nearly all species of snake the females are larger than the males.

Grass snakes are egg-layers. They emerge from hibernation in April, if it is sunny enough, and mate soon after. The eggs are usually laid about two months after mating. A full-grown female will lay between thirty and forty eggs; a younger one from eight to ten; the record recorded clutch is fifty-three. A manure heap is a favourite nesting place and snakes come back to the same place year after year. Any patch of rotting vegetation where warmth is generated will do, piles of sawdust, or hay ricks. Grass snakes have even been known to lay their eggs in holes in the walls of village houses so as to get the warmth from the old baking-ovens. According to Malcolm Smith the only other European snake that nests in places where warmth is artificially generated is the Aesculapian snake (*Elaphe longissima*).

The female grass snake burrows into the heap and then rolls herself into a ball and forms a chamber in which she lays the eggs, taking from ten to twelve hours on the job, ejecting eggs at first in quick succession, later more slowly. Quite often several females choose the same manure heap in which to lay their eggs, and as all the eggs hatch out at about the same time you soon hear talk of a plague of grass snakes. I know of one of these, but I shall not reveal the area because with grass snakes retailing at nearly £2 apiece the temptation for dealers might be too great. The eggs are less than an inch long, soft coated, leathery. The proportion of fertile eggs is high. Incubation takes from six to ten weeks. The young bash their way out with a special egg-tooth that afterwards disappears. They are 6 or 7 inches long, perfectly formed and very active. Nobody seems as yet to have discovered precisely what they feed on at this stage. The grass snake's predators include hedgehogs and some say badgers. Birds eat the young. Herons have been seen with quite sizeable adult snakes in their beaks.

Copulation is performed in the usual ophidian way: the male and female snakes entwine together and open their anal scale plates. It is possible that grass snakes also have a habit of twining together in clusters of three. I remember very vividly the first grass snakes I ever saw. They were in a hedge near a pond in a quiet field above Otterton in Devonshire, a county where grass snakes though not uncommon are not exactly abundant. I was twelve and very excited. My companion X, two years older, who knew of my herpetological fervour, had come upon a grass snake there quite by chance the day before. He guided me to the place. We left our bicycles in the lane close by and crept into the field. The snakes, three of them, according to my recollection, were entwined in what seemed to me a pattern, but I didn't have much time to look at it because X, who had picked up a stick, let out a yell: 'The swine!' and struck them. He thought they were copulating and the sight was too much for his Lowland Scots puritan conscience. One snake was killed; one, I think, escaped into the recesses of the hedge. The other I caught.

It has often occurred to me that I might have imagined that third snake, possibly for some unconscious reason. All I can say now is that I still don't think I did. I cannot be absolutely certain.

The snake I caught tamed readily. It didn't, as some grass snakes do, hiss or make mock strikes at me; nor did it sham dead like one I caught many years later in the New Forest which almost persuaded me to drop it in a clump of ferns. It did, however, let out that frightful grass snake's defensive stink from its anal glands. This has been

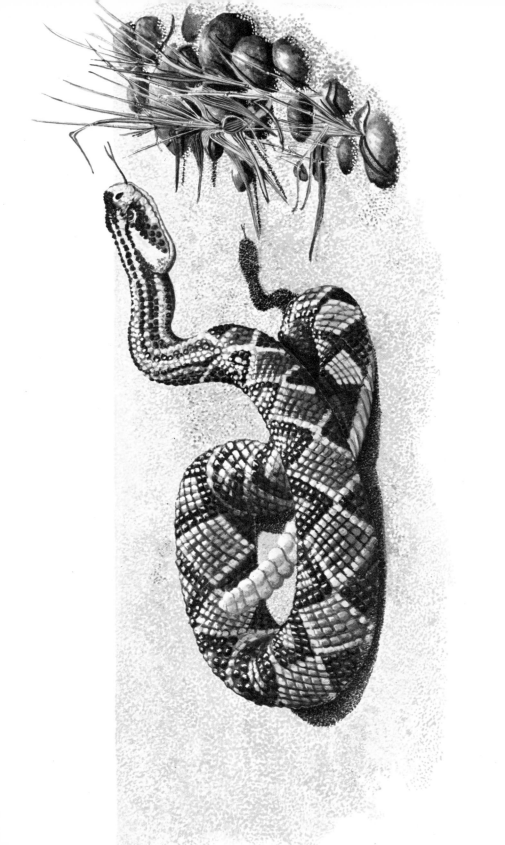

South American rattlesnake (*Crotalus durissus*). This large rattlesnake has the most powerful venom of all the species in its family. It was familiar to the ancient Peruvians, as you can see from their burial pits.

compared to rotten eggs and sulphuretted hydrogen, but it is subtler and more pervasive. It clings to the hands of the captor long after the captive is tamed and has stopped letting it off, and when he washes his hands it makes a new and even more noxious blend with the scent of the soap. I am told that the molecules of these evil-smelling secretions are related to the molecules of organic substances used in making expensive scent. It would be a very kinky scent-addict who used 'Essence of Grass Snakes' Anal Secretion'; I doubt if she would be popular at parties. Incidentally, the ability to let off the stink is present in the young grass snakes, as I know from experience, though the smell is fainter.

I rode my bicycle home in ecstasy with one hand, carrying the snake with the other, and we were chased by a hornet for several hundred yards on the way through Otterton Park. Quite an eventful little safari.

That night the snake escaped, pushing its head through a hole in the perforated zinc of an old meat safe. I think I know where it went, and if so I recaptured it, because during the next summer holidays I found a grass snake on a bank where I had never seen one before, though I had been there spring and summer year after year to catch lizards. And after catching that grass snake I never saw one there again, although the environment, with the bank at the edge of the wood and fields and a little stream close by, was just about right. To get to the bank it must have had to travel about half a mile and the first part of the trip was not easy – through several gardens with paling-fences and across the main Budleigh Salterton–Exmouth road.

The personality of a grass snake: can one use such a term? Yet snakes are quite sufficiently complex animals to have individual personalities. To paraphrase Gertrude Stein, 'Every grass snake is naturally alike and simply different.' The problem, insoluble I am afraid, is how to distinguish between the animal's real personality and the anthropomorphic fantasy qualities with which one invests it. A small boy's attitude to his pet snake is bound to be subjective. The first feel of the delicate flickering forked tongue on one's nose was interpreted by me as a benevolent caress. Most of the colubrine snakes I have handled have seemed to me to have a quality I would call *insouciance*.

It is, quite certainly, a temperamental snake and it is reputed to be very sensitive to violent thunderstorms. In Germany, according to Norman Douglas, if overtaken by a violent thunderstorm *Natrix* may be seen 'lying drowsy and benumbed by the roadside'. Douglas suggests this may be due to the sudden drop in temperature, several degrees in a minute.

The story I am now going to tell, if considered anthropo-morphically, might seem a story of extreme gallantry; considered scientifically I suppose it has to be classed as an instance of instinctive behaviour. It is true:

A young English male grass snake up in London from the country was in a dreadful predicament. His captor had sent him not to a pet-shop whence he might have fetched up in a schoolboy's pocket or a snug vivarium, but to the Hamadryad's larder in the Reptile House at the Zoo. The hamadryad, as we know, feeds exclusively on snakes, much prefers them live, and very often refuses them if they are dead. This hamadryad, a huge female 16 feet 9 inches long, was the pride and joy of the Reptile House. They were determined to keep her in full bloom.

The grass snake was introduced. The hamadryad reared up her head, spreading her hood a little. Her eyes didn't seem quite to focus on him at first; she flicked out her tongue. The grass snake was under 3 feet, a bit less than a fifth of her length. He showed no sign of fear. He wriggled over to the hamadryad's tail, twined round it, opened his anal scale plate and ex-truded one of his hemipenes, expecting her to receive him. The hamadryad lowered her head, peered intensely at him, flicking out her tongue. Then she seized him in her jaws and that was that. (Perhaps his was too noble a nature to sham dead, which might well have saved his life, rather than snatch the opportunity of a sensationally exciting act of love.)

The distribution of the smooth snake has always been limited to parts of Surrey, Hampshire and Dorset;[1] but a hundred years ago when Bournemouth was a village it was often seen in swarms. Now you have got to know exactly where to go and even then you will be lucky if you find one. (In 1955 I was staying at Brockenhurst and a New Forest official whom I met directed me to a pond on the road towards Beaulieu where he said smooth snakes had been seen. I think

[1] The first thing Norman Douglas said to me when I met him during the war and we started talking reptiles was: 'Have you ever caught a smooth snake?'

he was probably having me on, because when I got there there were so many paper bags and banana skins that no sensible snake would have gone near the place.)

Coronella is a small 2-foot-long, smooth-scaled, slim colubrine, light brown, greyish or even reddish above with rows of small ill-defined black or dark brown small spots on its back. It is sometimes mistaken for the adder, but any resemblance is merely superficial.

It likes dry, sandy, heath-type country with plenty of cover. It is mainly a lizard-eater and its favourite is the sand lizard (*Lacerta agilis*); their distributions overlap in places but do not quite coincide. It is one of the constricting colubrines and throws two or three coils round its prey before starting to swallow it. Reports about its suitability for captivity vary, but most authorities say it is difficult to feed. It is ovoviparous. Its young are born surrounded by membranes from which they break out. Rollinat, who observed the mating of smooth snakes, found that penetration was very deep and that one pair of snakes remained coupled for fifteen hours.

When I was writing this chapter I re-read Norman Douglas' *The Herpetology of the Grand Duchy of Baden*. In this he quotes an account by a Dr Settari who watched a *Coronella* feeding its young on lizards which it had eaten and regurgitated. This type of behaviour, common enough among birds, suggests a degree of parental care that is out of the question in reptiles. For a moment I was dumbfounded and then I noticed that Douglas went on to appear to have swallowed, and to be persuading his readers to swallow, the myth of adders swallowing their young. I remember that my old friend Professor Dawkins told me that Douglas had boasted to him playfully that he had set lots of little traps for his biographer after his own death. I feel quite sure that this must be such a trap, typical of Douglas' mischievous disposition. R. D. Lanworn, whom I consulted, suggests that Dr Settari (assuming him not to have been a figment of Douglas' imagination) might have observed a *Coronella* eating a lizard while its young, or one of them, was gobbling up the lizard's tail.

Why is *Coronella* so rare, or at any rate restricted, in England when on the continent of Europe it is one of the commonest snakes? It can't be the climate because it is found equally far north if not further, being even reported from Sweden. Presumably it is something to do with its preference for the sand lizard. The late and much lamented Jack Lester, Curator of the Reptile House, confessed to me that the specimen then on show with its habitat described as 'England' had been caught by him after a picnic in the forest of Fontainebleau.

Vipera berus, the common viper or adder, our only venomous snake and a very typical member of the subfamily *Viperinae*, is distributed very widely over the island, including Scotland. It is a small rather sturdy little snake generally not much over 2 feet, though in 1937 I saw one on the path beside the Sussex Ouse near Lewes that I could have sworn was close on 3 feet. The markings are unmistakable. There is a black V on the head and all the way down the back a thick black staring zig-zag pattern, so thick that it has been mistaken by many people, including Shakespeare in *A Midsummer Night's Dream*, for spots. The ground colour varies from light brown to dark brown to light grey. It is generally a safe bet to say that a grey adder is a male. The underbelly is a beautiful milky blue in the

Common viper or adder *(Vipera berus)*

females and black in the males. There are occasional melanistic or
black variations commoner in Europe than in Britain. The eye is
bright hazel with an elliptical pupil, a beautiful little eye. John
Aubrey compared it to the eye of Francis Bacon.

The viper likes a dry habitat, a heathery common or a bank at the
edge of a wood. It is very particular about its terrain. In one spot it
may teem; in another which you might think just as suitable you may
never see one. On Dartmoor it is fairly common in parts, but you are
supposed never to find it in a district where there are red ants. It is
less secretive than the grass snake and I once found one in a hedge at
the side of a main road in Devonshire. I was rather proud of spotting
this one, because I was sitting on the back of Ronald D'Alessio's
motor-bicycle. We stopped, caught it, took it into an open beech
wood at the foot of Knowle Hill and tested the number of times it
would strike at Ronald's dark blue silk handkerchief. It struck thirteen times and there was very little venom left after the first eight
strikes.

Vipers eat mice and the common lizards and occasionally young
birds. They are especially fond of the short-tailed field vole. They are
sometimes quite active at night; bustling little snakes, they make a
characteristic never-to-be-forgotten rustle as they move through dry
undergrowth.

As a rule they are timid and go for cover as soon as you approach
them. If you corner one and present it with a stick it will strike at it
defiantly. The nearest I have ever come to being attacked by an adder
was on a heathery patch of common near the first hole of the East
Devon Golf Course, which was ideal viper terrain — now all built
over. It was a hot afternoon at the end of April and a fine grey
specimen suddenly darted out between my feet and struck at the toe
of my sandshoe. I was thirteen at the time, still in the adder-bashing
stage, so I brought my stick down on him. That afternoon in an area
of 2 or 3 acres one other boy and I killed six adders. I skinned them
and kept the skins with my ties but somehow never got around to
wearing them.

The adder's striking movement is very quick. The mouse or lizard
is generally overpowered by the venom in a few seconds. The adder
will flick its tongue over it, then swallow it at leisure, beginning

with the nose. One adder I killed vomited out first, a newly swallowed vole, then a partially digested one, and then the remains of two more.

The venom is haemotoxic, affecting the blood stream and capillaries, causing acute local inflamation. The severity of the bite depends, as always, on where and how the fangs strike and how full the venom glands are at the time. An adder's bite can be exceedingly painful and may put a man out of action for a fortnight or three weeks, but it is very seldom fatal. There were seven deaths from adder bites between 1899 and 1945 (in England, Scotland and Wales); there has been one death since 1960. The number of demands for antivenene serum is around 400 per year, which suggests a fairly large number of bites, though some of these may be on dogs or even cattle. A committee appointed by the British Red Cross Society and the Royal Society of Tropical Medicine and Hygiene published a report in September 1962 which made the extraordinary statement that the bite of the adder, *Vipera berus*, is 'Less dangerous than is the use of antivenom . . .' For a fuller discussion of this the reader is referred to *Men and Snakes* by Ramona and Desmond Morris, pages 101–2. The first part of the report gave sensible instructions on first aid for snake bite, which in the case of adder bites can be condensed as follows:

The commonest symptoms are fright. Convincing reassurance is vital. Keep the patient at rest. Apply a light constricting ligature using a handkerchief to occlude veins and lymphatics – but not the arteries. This must be released for one minute in every thirty. Wash the bitten surface with clean water without rubbing. Immobilise the bitten part as for a fracture. Administer analgesics such as aspirin – but not morphia or, presumably, any preparation containing a morphine derivative.

There is still some controversy about the advisability of cutting the skin and then sucking the wound. Most authorities now are in favour of sucking without cutting.

The adder, as I have indicated, may be quite thick on the ground. It is recorded that 2400 were killed on a reclamation site of 60 acres in Scotland in a few years. Most bites are due to people treading on adders or picking them up. The most extraordinary case of an adder bite I ever read of was a naval petty officer who was climbing a cliff near Cawsand, just across the Cornish border beyond Plymouth. He lost his footing and clutched at a tuft of heather and gorse. It bore his weight all right, but he had got his hand round a live adder as well.

Adders congregate in swarms of a hundred or more in late autumn to hibernate, and emerge in early spring. "Tis the bright day that brings forth the adder', remarks Brutus in his garden in Shakespeare's *Julius Caesar*. True enough in spring, though in August a close sultry day with the sky overcast seems to bring them forth more readily, in my experience, than the blaze of noon. Basking adders generally stretch themselves out, though they may sometimes coil up neatly like a little spotted seaman's rope.

Vipera berus is viviparous; the young, about ten to fifteen of them, are surrounded by a membrane while inside the mother's body and break out of it at birth. There is a fair amount of courtship before mating — tongue-flickering and chin-nudging by the male. There is also a lot of ritual fighting between young male adders. Two of them will rear up several inches from the ground and press their necks against each other. No damage is done, but eventually the winner bears down on the loser very like a wrestler. The loser creeps away. The winner may then start courting a young female who has been coiled up close by. (Has she been smugly watching the duel for her affections?) Similar wrestling has been observed, as noted elsewhere in this book, among other snakes, notably rattlesnakes, and among colubrines such as the North American corn snake. Sir Julian Huxley in his delightful, recently published *Memories* describes witnessing, in the wooded crater of Astroni near Cumae, 5-foot-long black colubrines engaged in the ritual ceremonies.

The fable that the female adder in time of danger opens her mouth and swallows her young for their protection is widespread among rustics. Some of the accounts are weirdly circumstantial. The late Dr Malcolm Smith in his classic work *The British Amphibians and Reptiles* quotes an account by William Harrison that appears in Holinshed's Chronicle for 1577:

I did see an adder once myselfe that laie (as I thought) sleaping on a moule-hill, out of whose mouth came eleven yoong adders of twelve or thirteen inches in length apiece, which plaied to and fro in the grass one wyth another, tyll some of them espyed me. So soone therefore as they sawe me they ran againe into the mouth of theyr damme whome I killed, and then founde eache of them shrowded in a distinct celle or pannicle in hyr belly much like unto a soft white jelly.

This is a nice example of fact and fantasy. The unborn adders in their membranes are accurately described. The emergence of the young adders from their mother's mouth and return to it is of course total invention. The persistence of this myth is extraordinary. The suggestion that the rationalisation of it is provided by somebody witnessing the birth of young adders which, being viviparous, emerge live and active, is beside the point because in North America the same myth of swallowing and regurgitation of young snakes by their mother is attributed to several egg-laying species.

Who preys on the adder? Hedgehogs certainly; these, apart from the protection of their spines, have a surprising degree of immunity to the venom. There are stories of buzzards swooping down on adders and tearing them apart with their claws. A more surprising predator, though not so much in Britain where it is confined, is the pig. Pigs have not only tough hides but thick layers of fat underneath them which stop the snake's venom from getting into their blood. The common viper is child's play to a pig, which can cope with a really long-fanged viperid like the *fer de lance*. Also pigs appear to have an instinctive knowledge of just how to deal with vipers. They don't waste time sniffing at them and risking a bite on their tender snouts. They rush at them and trample them to death. In the scrubby oak-uplands of Estremadura, that primitive part of eastern Spain near the Portuguese frontier, famous also for its villages of imbeciles, vipers abound. The pigs, which are turned loose, feed on them and thrive. The viper-fed ham of Estremadura is said to be superior in flavour, subtler and more tangy, to the peach-fed ham of Virginia. I believe you used to be able to get it at Fortnum and Mason's. So perhaps there is something in the wonderful properties attributed to viper's fat by doctors and apothecaries until, at any rate, the beginning of the nineteenth century. In the summer of 1967, when staying in Fontainebleau, I was told that viper soup was still eaten by some of the peasants in forest villages. Next time I go there I hope to try it.

Vipera berus has several interesting European cousins and I must give them some space to themselves. There are altogether seven species in Europe including *V. berus*. All have the distinctive black zig-zag along the back.

There is *vipera aspis*, the 'aspic' about which French country women carry on so, crediting it with the ability to jump up and bite them in the face; true, it does sometimes move by sidewinding. It is seldom if ever found north of Paris. *V. aspis* is slightly larger than *V. berus*. Its body colour varies and some individuals have a distinctly red tinge. Its nose is very slightly turned up. It often half buries itself in soft soil when lying in wait for its prey. The sand viper (*Vipera ammodytes*) inhabits parts of Bavaria and Austria, Italy and the Balkans. It is appreciably larger than the common viper and grows to 3 feet and more. Its nose turns up so sharply that it looks like a little horn. It has particularly large fangs for a smallish viper, and potent venom. It has the reputation of being rather sluggish, but this may be based on its behaviour in captivity. It can snap up a 5-inch lizard in two minutes.

There is an Iberian species, *Vipera latastii*, in Spain and Portugal which has a turned-up snout like the sand vipers but not quite so exaggerated. In Greece there is *Vipera lebetina*, largest of the European vipers, possibly a closer relation of the imposing Palestinian viper (see p. 95).

The most endearing, certainly, of the European vipers is Orsini's viper (*Vipera orsinii*) found in south-central Europe, south-eastern France, northern Italy and Yugoslavia. It looks very like the common viper, though its head is a little narrower. Orsini's viper appears to be well equipped with venom glands and fangs, but it is exceptionally gentle and has never been known to bite. It is a favourite with children. There is another closely allied species, *Vipera orsinii macrops*, so called because of its large eyes. This snake has given up the use of its fangs and venom altogether and taken to a diet of grasshoppers, on which it gorges itself to repletion. It too is extremely gentle. So far as is known this is a unique case.

The distinctive markings of the viper have given rise to a lot of speculation about 'purpose' in evolution, much of it superstitious. It is suggested that venomous species are sharply marked as a warning to other animals to keep clear of them. This may be the relic of a religious attitude such as you find in the writings of some Victorian naturalists, who suggest that a benevolent creator labelled poisonous snakes as dangerous; and to this day American fundamentalists will assure you that it was God who fixed the rattle on the rattlesnake's tail. Actually, as has been mentioned elsewhere, it is extremely difficult to distinguish between many venomous and nonvenomous species.

Chapter 11

The Chelonians: Tortoises and Turtles

There are some 240 or so known living species in that also ancient and venerable Order, the *Chelonia*. And when you consider the similarity of the basic pattern, with each individual enclosed in a hard shell, toothless jaws with a horny beak, vestigial tails, etc, it is really rather remarkable how much diversity there is in size and habitat. There are land chelonians, aquatic and marine forms, and variations in size from the huge marine turtles and the hefty tortoises of the Galapagos Islands, to the tiny terrapins that would fit into a soap dish.

The Order is indeed ancient. Fairly typical chelonians appear in the late Triassic period about 200 million years ago, since when they are thought to have remained relatively unchanged. A small fossil reptile *Eunotosaurus*, from the Permian, about 300 million years ago may have been near the main trunk of the chelonian family tree. Its ribs had begun to form a sort of carapace.

The typical features of chelonians, common to all living species, can be briefly summarised. The shell is made up of two layers, the outer of horny scale-plates, the inner of bone. The dorsal ribs are fused with the shell. The neck, as if to compensate for the rigidity of the body, is very mobile. There are special features of the articulation of the shoulder and pelvic girdles, governed by the shell and its development. There is no sternum and the chest cannot be distended. For some time the problem of chelonian respiration was unsolved; but in 1863 Mitchell and Moorhouse showed that inspiration is done by a contraction of the oblique abdominal muscles at the hindleg pockets; this expands the lung cavities. Expiration is done by the ventral abdominal muscles, which deflate the lungs by pushing the viscera against them. Some freshwater turtles have a most ingenious supplementary system of respiration; the vascular mucous membranes of the gullet, and also the cloaca, act as gills and filter oxygen from the water. These turtles can stay under water for several days.

Sight is quite good, likewise sense of smell. Hearing is thought to be dull, though there are variations. During mating chelonians make barking and grunting noises. The male has one penis inside the cloaca at the base of the tail. Females may be larger than males, twice as large in some species. Courtship among tortoises may consist of butting and some biting of the female by the male; but in some turtle species, *Chrysemys* and *Pseudemys*, it is quite complicated, almost lyrical. The male swims backwards in front of the female and strokes her face with his elongated front claws. The eggs are laid in holes dug in earth or rotten vegetation (tortoises), or in sand (turtles). The number of eggs laid vary from one in one species of tortoise (*Testudo tornieri*) to 200. The eggs are leathery, typically reptilian.

The longevity of chelonians is unquestionably greater than that of any other reptiles, but accurate statistics are rather hard to come by and practical-jokers amuse themselves by carving little legends such as 'Testudo Cicero, natus A.U.C. DCCI amicus carus Julii Caesari' on the backs of the shells of live specimens. There seem to be authenticated cases of two members of *Testudo graeca* living to a century or so, and there is the large tortoise on a Pacific island which may have been living towards the end of the eighteenth century when Captain Cook paid him a visit.

The record weight for the giant *Testudo* of the Galapagos Islands is 560 lbs. Some of the marine turtles are very much larger. The leather-back turtle (*Dermochelys coriacea*) is enormous: over 7 feet long, 12 feet wide across the front paddles and weighing more than 1500 lbs. For a chelonian, the advantages of marine life, with seawater to take some of the weight of its shell, and the easy, swift mobility that flipper-swimming affords, seem very great. To lead the life of a land tortoise must require the temperament of a Diogenes.

The nomenclature of the chelonians is somewhat bedevilled by the American use of the word 'turtle' for a number of land species which the English call tortoise. The following is a simplified classification.

The Order *Chelonia* is divided into a number of superfamilies, families and subfamilies, the great majority of which are grouped

Galapagos giant tortoise *(Testudo elephantopus)*

under a single suborder *Cryptodira*, in which the neck is retracted in a vertical bend and the pelvis is not fused to the shell. Here is a selection of the more important families:

SUPERFAMILY TESTUDINOIDEA: this includes the following.

Subfamily *Chelydrinae*: large big-headed predacious turtles of North America. A typical genus is *Macrohelys*, the 'alligator-snapping turtle', one of the largest freshwater turtles.

Subfamily *Emydinae*: most of the smaller terrapins (sometimes called water tortoises in England) and a few larger forms.

FAMILY TESTUDINIDAE: these are the land tortoises with shells that are mostly domed, digits unwebbed with strong claws. Among them are the common European tortoise (*Testudo graeca*) and the Galapagos giant (*T. elephantopus*).

SUPERFAMILY CHELONIOIDEA: by far the most important subdivision of this lot is the *Cheloniidae*.

Family *Cheloniidae*: this contains all the living sea-turtles except *Dermochelys*. The limbs are paddle-shaped with one or two claws. The genera are very widely distributed, all over the warmer seas of the world. Conspicuous species include the green turtle (*Chelonia mydas*), the hawk-billed turtle (*Eretmochelys imbricata*) and the loggerheads – *Lepidochelyus kempi* in the Atlantic and *L. olivacea* in the Pacific and Indian Oceans.

FAMILY TRIONYCHIDAE: these are specially adapted for freshwater life, flattened 'soft-shelled' turtles in which the outer, horny, shell is absent and the inner, bony, shell much reduced. The nose is elongated into a snout.

The Suborder *Plenodira* is a somewhat younger order than the *Cryptodira*. The bones are more closely joined to the skull. All its members are aquatic. The principal family is the *Chelyidae*, who are all confined to the Southern Hemisphere. Members include the Australian snake-necked turtles of the genus *Chelodina* and a number of South American species.

The chelonian shell is a most remarkable piece of biological engineering – if I may borrow Dr Bellairs' expressive phrase. It must have a note to itself. It may amount to 30 per cent or more of the total weight. As a defensive armour it is unique. The nearest approach to it among other reptiles is the carapace of some extinct forms. In mammals it has a close analogue in the light armour suits of the armadillos.

The shell consists of two parts. The carapace above and the plastron below. They are joined together on either side between the legs by a bridge which is mainly the product of the plastron. The shell does not fully develop until after the young chelonian has hatched from its egg; calcium is plainly an essential part of the chelonian diet.

Shell structure is very varied among the different families. Some tortoises have developed hinges across the plastron and these, when head, limb and tail have been withdrawn, can be compared to a drawbridge which completes the isolated fortification of the castle. In the species of African tortoise, *Kinixys erosa*, the plastron projects into a ram. Presumably this is an offensive weapon, for *Kinixys* has been observed using it in attempts to turn other tortoises over on their backs. The general combination of impregnability with the chelonian's low metabolic rate and the even tenor of its way of life should provide a formidable survival value. Yet such are the vagaries of evolution that we find in a few forms that phenomenon of shell-reduction. This may be observed in some of the giant tortoises whose shells are thinner than might have been expected. The weight perhaps has proved too great. And there is one distinctly odd land tortoise, *Malacochersus tornieri,* in which the carapace is flat and feels strangely boneless. It has a flexibility that comes in handy for squeezing between rocks.

Marine turtles, with the support of seawater, are not troubled with the weight problem; but in some species the horny plates of the shell have degenerated, and in the soft-shelled turtles the carapace and plastron are covered with leathery skin only. Also lacking a horny outer shell is *Dermochelys coriacea*; its carapace is composed of a mosaic of tiny bones and is separate from the ribs and vertebrae.

Most chelonians, and all the tortoises, give you the impression that their skulls are at least big enough for them. There are several, however, of the terrapin or water tortoise brigade such as the Australian snake-necked water tortoise (*Chelodina longicollis*) which looks as if its carapace might have been added as an afterthought. There are few eccentric protuberances such as you find among the lizards, though several species have snouty ornamentations and one, *Chelys fimbriata,* has a miniature rhinoceros horn, also fleshy fringes on its mouth and neck which wave in the current and lure the fish.

Considering the limitations that you might expect the shell to impose, the movements of land tortoises are quite varied. They can climb a little and will go up a sloping tree trunk to find a suitable sunning place. When copulating, the male of *Terrapene carolina carolina,* the box turtle, assumes an upright sitting posture. A question that is often asked is why are the two giant tortoises, *T. elephantopus* and *T. gigantea,* only found on islands – Galapagos and Madagascar? What are the ecological reasons why these environments suit them so well? An extinct giant tortoise of sensational proportions, *Testudo atlas,* from northern India has a shell more than 6 feet long.

A most industrious chelonian is the gopher tortoise of the USA and Mexico. This digs elaborate burrows 40 or 50 feet long and 12 feet deep, to which it retires in numbers. Unconcernedly, no doubt, they share these burrows with a strange assortment of other animals, racoons, rattlesnakes, opossums.

Who are the predators – hominids excepted – of the chelonians? It is difficult to think of any animal that can be much of a threat to even a quite small tortoise, though a Malayan monitor once swallowed one whole by mistake. The legend of the death of Aeschylus, who is reputed to have been killed when nearing his hundredth birthday by a tortoise which was dropped on his head by an eagle, may be true; but there are no recorded instances of eagles letting tortoises fall from a height so that their shells may smash.

The eggs are much more vulnerable. Crocodiles and monitors dig them up by the score. Monitors will spend hours digging for turtles' eggs in the sand.

A curiosity worth noting is the little American musk-turtle (*Sternotherus carinatus*, generally known as the stinkpot). This is common, omnivorous and aggressive. It lets off a smell that is even nastier and more clinging than that of the grass snake. Whom is this intended to repel?

The diet of chelonians is immensely varied. Many of the land tortoises appear to be strictly vegetarian; nobody seems to know why. The marine forms eat any sort of sea food they can get their beaks into, from squid to sea snakes.

A particularly voracious and omnivorous species is the American snapping turtle, which is very unpopular with wildfowlers because of its penchant for ducks and its ability to steal up to the surface of the water and snap them down. It will also eat snakes. It has an uncanny nose for flesh. Clifford H. Pope tells a story of an Indian who kept a snapping turtle on a string and hired it out to the local law when a missing person was thought to have been drowned. As a corpse-retriever it was infallible.

A word or two about the sea turtles. In these few species the chelonians are seen at their brilliantly adapted best. A large land tortoise roaring along on the flat may reach a speed of $\frac{1}{4}$-$\frac{1}{2}$ mph. A marine turtle can certainly swim at 15 knots per hour and possibly

Long-nosed tree snake (*Dryophis nasuta*). A native of Malaya and Indonesia, the long-nosed tree snake is one of the mildly venomous back-fanged snakes. Fantastically slender and attenuated, it is a master of camouflage.

Snapping turtle (*Macrohelys temmincki*)

a lot more. Such mobility implies a fuller life. If only more were known . . .

The green turtle (so called because of the colour of its fat), *Chelonia mydas*, is the edible species, remorselessly pursued by greedy men. Its shell is 46 inches long and it may weigh 850 lbs; it stays in tropical waters. It eats seaweed and algae, jellyfish, molluscs and crustaceans. It likes to sun itself. The female of *C. mydas* lays up to 200 eggs in the sand. On moonlight nights you can see scores of them coming out of the sea to land on the little islands of North-west Borneo, struggling ponderously up the beach to deposit the eggs above the high-water mark. The effort involved is enormous and the sighs which female turtles emit on these occasions are a real expression of distress and the need for air; respiration[1] on land is twice as laborious as at sea, partly owing to weakness in the bridges between carapace and plastron. Next morning the females return to the sea, and the males, who are lying in wait for them ('Like ponces outside

[1] The practice of turning captive green turtles over on their backs, which you may have seen in films, is not just a piece of extra brutality; they do breathe better that way.

a lying-in hospital', as an Irish sailor said to me), immediately mate with them.

There are signs that the green turtle is in danger of becoming, if not extinct, at least very seriously reduced in numbers, so high has the rate of capture become. It is a docile species and could be readily tamed if time could be spared from eating it.

The hawksbill turtle (*Eretmochelys imbricata*) is also unfortunate because it is the chief provider of tortoiseshell. Its plates are translucent and especially suitable for carving. It got a bit of a reprieve earlier in this century when celluloid and other plastics came in, but the demand for real tortoiseshell is again strong. The East Indian islands, Ceylon and also the Caribbean are the breeding grounds of this fine and rather ferocious chelonian. It is a good deal smaller than the green turtle, only some 30 inches in shell length.

The loggerhead (*Caretta caretta*) is big; 36 inches shell length and a weight of 300 lbs is common; weights of 900 lbs have been recorded. Some optimistic authorities hint at the possibility of bigger giants than this, for the loggerhead is carnivorous and insatiable. Its own flesh tastes nasty and is very stringy, but its eggs are good eating. It has a bad temper. Also it is a hardy species and very widespread. In the Atlantic it will nest as far north as Virginia and has been sighted cruising off Nova Scotia.

Also called 'loggerheads' are two species of sea turtle known as the 'Ridleys', Atlantic and Pacific. *Lepidochelys kempi* is the Atlantic Ridley, smallest of sea turtles, shell barely 2 feet. It is confined to the Gulf of Mexico and not much is known about it except that it becomes furious when captured, snapping its beak continually. The Pacific Ridley, *L. olivacea*, is rather larger and ranges along the coast of South America from Chile to Mexico. It is part vegetarian. The female when laying her eggs, after the usual laborious calvary from sea to high-water mark, sheds copious tears to keep the sand from her eyes. (She does not, like the 'Mock-turtle' in *Alice in Wonderland*, brush them aside with her flipper.)

The leather-back sea turtle (*Dermochelys coriacea*) belongs, as has been mentioned, to a family of its own because of the peculiar structure of its shell. This is a giant among chelonians and the heaviest living reptile. A weight of 1200 lbs is not uncommon, with a width

Chicken turtle (*Deirochelys reticularia*)

from flipper to flipper of 12 feet. The flippers are clawless but immensely powerful with the foreflippers longer than the hind. The young of the leather-back are quite brightly coloured,[1] with white or yellow spots. The egg-laying performances are quite epic and involve, together with floods of tears, an immense amount of sand-scattering.

[1] There are several brightly coloured chelonians. To mention a few, the painted turtle (*Chrysemys picta*) has a beautiful dark blue body with red and yellow and white stripes. The wood turtle (*Chlemys insculpta*) has a terracotta neck. This is the turtle which is supposed to be on a par with a rat for finding its way through a maze. The spotted turtle (*Chlemys fullata*) is lightly spattered over head and shell with light primrose spots and its legs have pink stripes. There are also admirable shell patterns to be observed among tortoises, the star tortoise (*Testudo elegans*) being one of the most pleasing with its complex pyramidal alternation of palest yellow and darkest brown.

Chapter 12

The Crocodilians

Classification may seem tedious, yet it is necessary and useful, like a list of historical dates by which you orientate yourself. In the case of the *Crocodilia* it is mercifully simple because there are only twenty-six species divided into three families: the *Alligatoridae*; the *Crocodylidae*; the *Gavialidae*.

The entire group is but a handful of survivals from the great age of reptiles. Among the crocodilians of those days, when reptiles ruled the world, were genuine monsters like *Phobosuchus* with a 6-foot-long skull and a 45-foot-long body; and *Rhamphosuchus*, a giant Indian gavial whose fossil remains date from the Pliocene. These became extinct along with the dinosaurs. Meanwhile crocodiles very like the living species appeared in the Triassic period.

Our three families are very similar and differences between them — over length, width of snout and arrangement of scales — are less than those between the families of snakes or lizards.

All crocodilians are amphibious and riparian, inhabiting the banks of rivers, lakes and swamps. They are more at home in water, but they can move fast on land, generally in short rushes. Their tails are flattened into paddles; when they swim they tuck their legs in close to their bodies. They are all egg-laying and sun-loving. They often assemble in masses and make an impression — possibly misleading — of gregariousness.

All are heavily armour-plated. There are several ingenious adaptations for the aquatic life. The throat has a valve that closes it tight, and there is a passage from the nostrils opening into the windpipe behind the throat-valve. The nostrils also have valves; the eyes have upper and lower lids and a nictitating membrane; the eyesight is good. The crocodile can therefore submerge without flooding its respiratory passage even when its mouth is held half open by the prey which it has siezed in its jaw and is dragging under water. The ear is protected by scaly flaps. The heart is completely partitioned and there is no mixture of arterial and venous blood as in other reptiles. There is a partition between the thoracic and abdominal cavities somewhat like the diaphragm in mammals. The oesophagus can be expanded and used for storing food, though the crocodile has such powerful teeth and neck and jaw muscles that it can easily tear its prey to pieces. There is a muscular gizzard in which bony fragments are found. The cloacal opening is a longitudinal slit. The male has a single penis. The female crocodilian has a small clitoris. The male has glands in the throat and cloaca which release a musky secretion.

Crocodile courtship consists of roaring, and the female is thought to answer back in a duet; the female Nile crocodile has been seen flirting, rearing up out of the water with her jaws wide open. Male alligators rub their heads along the females' backs. Copulation takes place under water and lasts for fifteen minutes. Males in the breeding season become savagely aggressive and fight seriously, without any ritual bluff, sometimes to the death. . . . But we must return to classification:

The family *Crocodilidae* consists of fifteen species. Most of them inhabit the Old World. Here they are:

Species	Range	Length, feet
West African dwarf crocodile (*Osteolemus tetraspis*)	West Africa	5–6
Congo dwarf crocodile (*Osteolemus osborni*)	Congo basin	$3–3\frac{3}{4}$
Nilotic crocodile (*Crocodylus niloticus*)	Africa and Madagascar	12–16
African slender-snouted crocodile (*Crocodylus cataphractus*)	Congo basin to Senegal	6–8
Mugger (*Crocodylus palustris*)	Southern Asia, India	10–13
Siamese crocodile (*Crocodylus siamensis*)	South-east Asia and Java	10–12

Species	Range	Length, feet
New Guinean crocodile (*Crocodylus novae-guineae*)	New Guinea	8–9½
Australian crocodile (*Crocodylus johnstoni*)	Australia	6–8
Mindoro crocodile (*Crocodylus mindorensis*)	Philippines	5–8
Saltwater crocodile (*Crocodylus porosus*)	Southern Asia, Indonesia and Australia	12–20
American crocodile (*Crocodylus acutus*)	North-western South America, Central America, Mexico, West Indies and Florida	10–23
Cuban crocodile (*Crocodylus rhombifer*)	Cuba	6–8
Morelet's crocodile (*Crocodylus moreleti*)	Mexico and Central America	6–7
Orinoco crocodile (*Crocodylus intermedius*)	Orinoco basin	10–23
False gavial (*Tomistoma schlegeli*)	Malay peninsula	9–16

The family *Gavialidae* has only one species:

Indian gavial	Southern Asia	12–21

Finally the family *Alligatoridae*:

Broad-nosed caiman (*Caiman latirostris*)	Brazil and Paraguay	6–6¾
Paraguay caiman (*Caiman yacare*)	Paraquay	6–8
Spectacled caiman (*Caiman sclerops*)	Amazon and Orinoco basins	6–8
Central American caiman (*Caiman fuscus*)	Mexico, Central America and Colombia	4–6
Black caiman (*Melanosuchus niger*)	Amazon basin and Guianas	10–15
American alligator (*Alligator mississippiensis*)	South-eastern United States	8–19

Species	Range	Length, feet
Chinese alligator (*Alligator sinensis*)	Eastern China	4–6½
Smooth-fronted caiman (*Paleosuchus trigonatus*)	Amazon basin	4–4
Dwarf caiman (*Paleosuchus palpebrosus*)	Amazon basin	3½–4

Alligators and caimans have broad, rounded snouts, whereas the snouts of most crocodiles tend to be longer and more pointed. In alligators the fourth tooth of the lower jaw fits into a pit in the upper jaw; in the crocodiles it projects outside. The gavial and the false gavial are marked off from all other crocodilians by their long and exaggeratedly slender snouts. Male gavials have a swelling on the tip of the snout, function unknown. Alligators are freshwater dwellers and keep away from saltwater. Some crocodiles seem to like brackish water. The saltwater crocodile makes long voyages.

No one knows how long crocodiles live in their natural state. Their age in captivity has not always been accurately recorded. Major S. S. Fowler, who made an intensive study of the subject, found authenticated ages of at least thirty-three for alligators. Ferocity and danger to man vary greatly. Here are some notes on individual species.

The African crocodile (*C. niloticus*) is the classical crocodile of antiquity described at length by Herodotus though not altogether accurately; not only was he confused by the wide-open mouth into thinking that the lower jaw must be articulated to the skull. He also alleged that the crocodile had no tongue. Aristotle – perhaps he had never seen a crocodile – repeated the fallacy. Herodotus did correctly observe the Nile plover hopping in and out of the gaping jaws of a row of crocodiles, picking their teeth for them. *C. niloticus* likes saltwater and swims freely. In ancient days it even ventured into the eastern Mediterranean and came ashore on the coast of Palestine.

Making every allowance for exaggeration it does seem that *C. niloticus* is inclined to attack human beings. The evidence varies. In some villages the natives have built stockades at the edge of the river to protect the women when they come to fill their water-jars. In others, as Inger remarks, the children splash about and no harm comes to them. It has been suggested that some aged crocodiles may become addicted to human flesh somewhat like man-eating tigers; doubtful, one feels. But there is no question whatever about the aggressiveness of *C. niloticus*. Attacks, as vicious as they were un-provoked, have been made on canoes and particularly of late on outboard motorboats – almost as if the phut-phutting of their engines was interpreted as some territorial challenge. Sometimes *C. niloticus* becomes so enraged that it charges down the bank, plunges in and swims towards a boat, opening and shutting its jaws in a shower of spray. The scene, not in the least exaggerated, is one with which most of us are familiar from the covers of boys' papers. American zoologists have vividly described an attack by a large crocodile when they were crossing a lake in Rhodesia in a rowboat. *C. niloticus* overturned the boat and stayed to savage the wreck with its jaws and thus gave them time to swim ashore.

Equally if not more savage is the saltwater crocodile *C. porosus.* (It is anatomically distinguished by the absence of the occipital scutes, rows of enlarged plates at the back of the head.) The odysseys of *C. porosus* are impressive. Not only does it swim from island to island in the Malay archipelago; it has been known to stray as far as the Fiji Islands in the Pacific and the Cocos Islands in the Indian Ocean, wanderings that must have entailed voyages of a thousand miles or more. In New Guinea during World War Two Captain Philip J. Darlington (jnr), an entomologist serving with the US Army Medical Corps, was savagely attacked by what is thought to have been a salt-water crocodile. He was collecting mosquito larvae for work on malaria control, standing on a log in a swamp, when he saw a croco-dile about 10 feet long rising through the water at his feet. He slipped and fell into the water and as he rose to the surface the croco-dile seized him by the arm and then did the usual crocodile trick of rolling over while backing into deep water, dragging its quarry with it. Darlington kicked and struggled and managed to break loose, sustaining a broken arm and some nasty lacerations. The female *S. porosus* makes a nest of vegetation and lays up to sixty eggs which she guards by basking on top of them. Incubation takes ten weeks.

The mugger (*Crocodylus palustris*) may be familiar to many readers

False gavial *(Tomistoma schlegeli)*

from Kipling's story 'The Mugger of Mugger Gaut'. Kipling exaggerates its size (13 feet is the absolute maximum) and its ferocity. In India it has a good reputation for not attacking humans, though Dr Derniyagala, the renowned Singhalese authority, says that in Ceylon the muggers are sometimes ferocious. The mugger is venerated by both Hindus and Moslems. Near Karachi some fifty muggers have been kept in sacred captivity in memory of a Moslem saint whose tomb is close by. Sometimes, when its marshy home dries up the mugger buries itself in the mud to wait for the rains.

The Indian gavial (*Gavialis gangeticus*) has a reputation for diffidence. It seldom attacks man, and though ornaments such as bracelets are quite often found in its stomach these are thought to have belonged to corpses floating in the river. The long slim snout of the gavial (and the 'false' gavial), which at a glance looks useless, if decorative, is well adapted for catching fish.

The American crocodile (*C. acutus*) is, like other species, becoming scarcer owing to unrestrained hunting. Schmidt describes a 'Crocodilian paradise' in northern Honduras, Lake Ticamaya, where he counted seventy-five specimens in one little marshy bay. Its domestic habits include the careful excavation of a nest and egg-laying in two neat rows; alas, signs of cannibalism have also been detected.

The American alligator[1] (*Alligator mississippiensis*) has an excellent reputation and is thought only to attack men if it is guarding a nest. E. A. McIlhenny in *The Alligator's Life History* describes how, as a boy in southern Louisiana, he and his friends used to swim up to young alligators and tease them. The only time he was attacked was when he was in a canoe. A 12-footer slid off the bank and upset the canoe with a stroke of its tail, another example of the irritant effect of small boats on crocodilians such as we saw in *C. niloticus*. Large specimens of the American alligator have been known to seize cows, pull them into the water and drown them. The rate of growth varies from about 9 inches a year. A 9 foot 2 inch male aged ten weighed 251 lbs. An 11 foot 6 inch specimen weighed 591 lbs. Although specimens of 19 feet and over have been recorded it is rare now to find one more than 12 feet long.

The American alligator digs deep holes 40 feet long which are usually partly waterlogged, in which it lies up during the winter. The process of building the nest as described by McIlhenny is quite elaborate. The female clears a space about 8 by 10 feet in a briar patch by biting off and trampling the branches. Then she makes a pile of vegetation, pushing it around with her snout and shoving it with her body. After that she makes a hollow in the centre of the heap and fills this with mud and plants gathered in her mouth. When the mound has been shaped to her satisfaction she lays the eggs. These she covers over with more mud and plants using her mouth. The finishing touch consists of crawling round and round the nest smoothing its surface and turning it into a surprisingly neat cone. The entire job, as observed, took three days and two nights.

Analysis of the contents of alligators' stomachs, nearly all from Louisiana, showed: 47 per cent crustaceans; 23 per cent insects and spiders; 29 per cent vertebrates, fishes, snakes, turtles, birds and

[1] The word alligator is derived from Spanish: *el lagarto*, the lizard.

mammals. As an example of the alligator's voracity, McIlhenny found, on opening the stomach of a 12-foot alligator, three pigs each weighing about 30 lbs.

McIlhenny conducted a rather dubious experiment with one alligator, making it bite a steel plate. All that happened was that the large teeth were pushed up through the poor old alligator's skull and had to be extracted from on top with pliers.

In spite of the alligator's great strength, and an ability to crush bones, it seems that its movements are somewhat limited and that it can be overpowered by surprise tactics. Perhaps the most remarkable attack by a man upon an alligator was made by the eccentric English nineteenth-century naturalist Charles Waterton. (Entertaining accounts of him are given in Norman Douglas's *Experiments* and Edith Sitwell's *English Eccentrics*.) Waterton was ever one for doing things the hard way. Suffering from a sprained ankle he treated it by holding it under Niagara Falls. In his *Wanderings in South America* he describes how he caught a fair sized caiman which he had observed from a canoe. He dived into the river, clung to the caiman's back, got his legs round it and pressed with his thumbs on its eyes. In its confusion the caiman allowed itself to be ridden ashore.

Waterton's feat has often been emulated in imagination by the writers of boys' adventure stories pounding away on their typewriters in Thames-side villas. He wouldn't have been successful with the giant black caiman (*Melanosuchus niger*) which ranges over the basins of the Amazon and Orinoco and reaches a length of 15 feet, or with the Orinoco crocodile which may be 20 feet long. Another herpetological subject for the writers of boys' books is the battle between the caiman or crocodile and an anaconda. No doubt the South American crocodilians do eat anacondas, though there do not seem to be any authentic eyewitness accounts. The odds would be heavily against the anaconda in a fight.

The Chinese alligator (*Alligator sinensis*) had for centuries figured in Chinese literature, and its bones and liver were in great demand in Chinese medicine, but its existence was not established by Western zoologists until 1879. In 1925 Clifford H. Pope collected nineteen specimens near the city of Wuhu up the Yangtse-Kiang River from Nanking. They were dug out from hibernation. It seems unlikely that

Chinese alligator *(Alligator sinensis)*

so comparatively small a species, only 5 feet long, should have been
the origin of Chinese preoccupation with dragons. Their habitat, with
increasing drainage and precautions against flooding, is likely to
become restricted. Let us hope that Chairman Mao will see fit to pre-
serve them.

And now, as the travelogue commentators say, we take our leave
of the ancient and venerable order of the *Crocodilia*, greatly in need
of care and protection. It would, as Dr Bellairs justly remarks, be 'a
tragedy if these last survivors of the great archosaurian dynasty were
to be exterminated just for the sake of a few more shoes and hand-
bags'. There is as yet no means of estimating any reptile's IQ, if
indeed the reptile cortex is developed enough to rate such a quotient.
But after even a brief acquaintance one finds it difficult not to believe
that there may be some foundation for the mythical sagacity with
which men have invested the *Crocodilia*. Perhaps there are shreds of
evidence that might suggest an intelligence superior to that of some

other reptiles: the elaborate nest-building; the keen interest which captive alligators show when their food is being got ready. On one thing we can congratulate them: though some species are more sluggish than others no single crocodilian in many millions of years has shown signs of degeneration. This is a proud record. Possibly the species that has done most to maintain it is the huge saltwater crocodile. This is the one with which I find it easiest to identify, not slouching in wait in the heavy daze of a tropical swamp, but swimming far and free in warm seas.

Chapter 13

Some Reptiles of North America

There are probably more herpetologists in the United States than in any other country. And this is not merely due to the size of the population; it does seem that educated Americans, as a group, take a considerable interest in the reptiles not only of their own country but of the world. Certainly this has been my experience when talking to my American friends and their children and with visiting Americans whom I have met in London and in the course of my travels. I note also that many of the best popular books about reptiles are by American writers such as R. L. Ditmars, and Schmidt and Inger.

Not only the alligators and turtles, which have been given chapters to themselves, but also most of the representative American species of lizards and snakes have been described elsewhere in this book and assigned to their places in the scheme of classification. This, of course, doesn't mean that there is not a great deal more to be said about them. Let us take the American lizards first. Of that interesting family the *Anguidae*, the legless lizards, there are several species found in the United States. The largest of them is the eastern glass 'snake' (*Ophisaurus ventralis*), which inhabits the Atlantic and eastern coastal plains. Its body is brown with darker strips along the back; it grows to more than 3 feet, two-thirds of which is tail. It likes woods and fields but sometimes burrows into the ground and is turned up when farmers are ploughing. It eats insects and earthworms, becomes very tame and will take food from the hand. It must be handled very carefully because its tail is brittle and easily broken off. It lays from four to seventeen eggs in a clutch.

Related to *Ophisaurus* are the alligator lizards found in Texas and along the Pacific coast. The largest is the Texas alligator lizard (*Gerrhonotus liocephalus*) at 20 inches. It has very short legs and a long prehensile tail which it uses when climbing. It is an egg-layer, but its close relation, the northern alligator lizard (*G. coeruleus*), is viviparous. Another family of legless lizards, the *Anniellidae,* are found in California. These are 8–10 inches long and specially adapted for burrowing. The only venomous lizards, the gila monster (*Heloderma suspectum*) found in Texas and Arizona, and its close relation the beaded lizard (*Heloderma horridum*) of western Mexico, have been described, together with their venomous properties, elsewhere (see p. 49).

Gila monster *(Heloderma suspectum)*

The most diverse family of lizards in the New World is the *Iguanidae.* There are some 700 species distributed from British Columbia in Canada to southern Argentina. Many of the lizards of North America belong to this family. They vary in size from the tiny Texas tree uta, 3–4 inches long, to the 7-foot iguanas of Mexico and Central South America. In all, four species of iguanids live in the USA, but of these only one species, the little Florida scrub lizard (*Sceloporus woodi*), is exclusive to the USA. The most widespread North American iguanid is the eastern fence lizard (*S. undulatus*). It is found from the Atlantic coast to Arizona and Utah. This is a pretty little lizard, especially the male, which has bright blue patches on its throat and belly. There are several more species in the drier country west of the Mississippi. The liveliest of these are the collared lizard (*Crotaphytus collaris*) and the leopard lizard (*C. wislizeni*). The collared lizard sometimes runs on its hindlegs like the basilisk of South America. If cornered it will face its pursuer and snap at him defiantly. A somewhat eccentric lizard is the Texas earless lizard (*Holbrookia Texania*) with a white tail with black bars under it. Sometimes it curls its tail and then waves it slowly in the air. Also iguanids are the horned 'toads', of the genus *Phrynosoma*, with spines on their heads and along their bodies, famous for their trick of squirting blood from their eyes when frightened.

'Most pleasing in aspect of all North American iguanids', according to the late Dr Karl P. Schmidt, one of the greatest of American herpetologists, is the desert iguana (*Dipsosaurus*), finely proportioned with a long tail and a little crest of scales along its back. It is about 15 inches long with a prettily marked back, greyish-brown with a reddish network. This and its cousin the chuckwalla (*Sauromalus*) inhabit the Great Basin and the Arizona and Mojave deserts. They climb creosote bushes to eat the leaves and flowers.

Like their African cousins, the agamids, none of the burrowing iguanids adapt themselves completely to subterranean existence and their limbs do not become shorter. Whether this is to be regarded as a sign of sturdy independence and refusal to degenerate the reader must decide for himself.

A number of iguanids can change colour and, as has been remarked elsewhere in this book, the *Anolis* family are often misnamed chamaeleons. Indeed that beautiful little American lizard *Anolis Carolinensis* is often sold in pet shops as a 'chamaeleon' and I have more than once had to reprove American friends who have told me that they have kept chamaeleons. What would I not give, as I sit here writing this chapter looking out over a typical English winter landscape where, if there is any reptile life at all, it is in deep hibernation, to be in a warm south-eastern state where these little living jewels are so relatively common.

Overcoming my unscientific prejudice against skinks, so widespread in both New and Old Worlds, I might draw your attention to some interesting American species such as the sand skink (*Neoseps reynoldsi*) of Florida, in which the eye has become very small and the

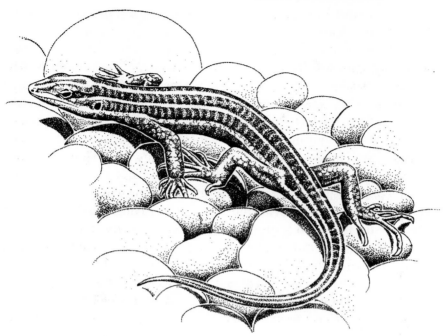

Five-lined skink *(Eumeces fasciatus)*

eyelid has thickened as part of adaptation to a burrowing life. The skinks, as has been mentioned, make use of their brittle tails as safety devices to divert predators. In two American species, the Pecos skink (*Eumeces taylori*) and the five-lined skink (*E. fasciatus*), the tails of the young – during that period when, as Schmidt points out, 'the hazards of life are greatest' – are bright blue. The five-lined skink is the commonest species in the eastern states. It is found in every state east of a line from Minnesota to Texas with the only exceptions being Vermont, New Hampshire and Maine. The little brown skink (*Lygosoma laterale*), occurring in southern New Jersey, Pennsylvania, Indiana, Missouri and eastern Texas, is of special interest as the only North American skink with a 'window' in its lower eyelid. The largest American skink is the great plains skink found in the southern half of the plains and in central Arizona with a length of a little over a foot.

The rattlesnakes, the chief herpetological glory of North America, have been described in some detail elsewhere (see p. 99), also the water moccasins and copperheads, and the only venomous colubrids of North America, the coral snakes. I have also dealt separately with some of my favourite American nonvenomous colubrids such as that interesting aggressive cannibal, the king snake. North America is rich in colubrid snakes. There are thirty-six genera and seven of these are viviparous. They range from the little red-bellied snake (*Storeria occipto-maculata*) which feeds on snails and slugs, and its cousin Dekay's snake, found in the suburbs of Chicago and New York, to the racers and the chicken snakes of the *Elaphe* genus. These latter include the handsome rat snakes, the black (*E. obsoleta*) and the yellow (*E. o. quadrivittata*). An interesting relation is the brown fox snake (*E. vulpina*) found as far north and west as Wisconsin and Nebraska. When confronted it coils up into a menacing posture and vibrates its tail rapidly, like a rattlesnake. There are also two beautiful green species, the smooth green snake (*Opheodrys vernalis*) and the rough green snake (*O. aestivus*) which is a tree-dweller.

The commonest North American snake, friend of schoolboys, is the beautiful striped garter snake (*Thamnophis*). There are several

Common garter snake *(Thamnophis cyrtopsis)*

species – for instance the black-necked garter snake (*T. cyrtopsis*) and the plains garter snake (*T. radix*) and the beautiful red and beige striped San Francisco garter snake (*T. sirtalis tetrataenia*). These elegant little snakes, all viviparous, form an interesting group midway between the land-living colubrines and the water snakes. Their distribution is wide and they are found in the northern United States and Canada. Some of the western species are as aquatic in their habits as the genus *Natrix*. The commonest North American *Natrix* is *N. sipedon*. The young of this species are brightly coloured with reddish-brown bands, rather more fetching to the eye than their English cousin, the olive-hued grass snake (*Natrix natrix*). Most of the American *Natrix* species share the family's defensive habit of emiting a foul-smelling anal secretion. One distinguished herpetologist has described this as 'musky'. This is surely one of the most optimistic descriptions of a stink on record.

The beauty of the North American colubrines should have been celebrated long ago by poets. The corn snake (*Elaphe guttata*) with its exquisite golden background for light mauve-brown spots with black rings is a particularly striking example. For elegance of form the racers take some beating; my favourites are the striped racer (*Coluber lateralis*) and the blue racer (*C. constrictor flaviventris*) common in the Middle West. Another splendid North American snake is the 8-foot-long indigo snake (*Drymarchon corais*). An eccentricity is the genus *Heterodon* comprising the three hog-nosed snakes of eastern North America. These are some of the colubrines that have adapted to the burrowing life. They have short thick bodies and keeled scales and feed principally on toads. The south-eastern species, which is the least common, has the most sharply upturned snout scale. All three species behave in a strange manner when confronted. They swell up and spread out their heads and necks, hiss and puff and strike in a most threatening manner. But if they are challenged and their bluff is called, they collapse and sham dead, lying limp on the ground with their bellies uppermost.

Another interesting North American colubrine is the rough earth snake (*Haldea straitula*), a small 10-inch viviparous species whose distribution ranges from Virginia to Texas. It is found under stones or tree bark and feeds mainly on earthworms. More specially adapted for burrowing, like the hog-nosed snakes, is the long-nosed snake (*Rhino cheilus*) of the south-western United States. The 4-foot-long Florida mud snake (*Faranci abacura*) is less 'deformed' for the obvious reason that mud does not offer so much resistance as dry soil. The mud snake is brightly coloured with red markings on a black background and has a hard, sharp tip at the end of its tail. It is the subject of various myths and superstitions, credited with being able to bowl itself along like a hoop; its tail is supposed – totally erroneously – to be a venomous sting.

Reptiles, especially snakes, are elusive creatures and even in tropical countries you see them less often than travellers' tales have lead you to expect. Often it is the children who spot them. My friend Mrs Marion Jopson tells me this about her herpetological adventures in that bright, flat, sunbaked state, Kansas, when she was a little girl of nine:

In summer there would be long dry spells. The ground would get parched and crack wide open. The only water was in the deep wells and muddy ponds. You could swim in these ponds so long as you never put a foot down except right near the edge. This was because big snapping turtles pottered about or lay on the bottom just waiting for food to come to them. When the water was low the boys would dare each other to walk across the pond in bare feet. And one boy did lose a toe. These were the same turtles that the Iroquois Indians used to make rattles with. The turtle symbolised longevity and great tenacity of life. The Iroquois believed that evil false faces, heads without bodies, appeared to people in the forest and bewitched them into sicknesses. The spell was only broken by a ceremony in which the Indians wore masks in the likeness of the false faces and for this a turtle rattle was used. The turtle was killed and hung up by the neck until the next day because it was said that no matter how early it was killed it would not die till sundown. Next day the head was severed from the neck and the heart and insides were removed. Then a stick was fitted in place of the neck and some dry corn put into the shell to make the rattle.

One day I and another little girl found a large black snake stretched out in a dried-up creek. I am pretty sure it was a water moccasin. My friend said it must be hungry because all the crayfish had gone back into the mud and it was too dry for frogs or fish. 'He'll sure die,' she said.

Our mothers had packed a picnic lunch for us, but we had eaten it all except one wedge of pumpkin pie. We stretched out over the edge of the creek and threw the pie down to the snake. It landed just in front of his head. We waited a long time and kept very still and, believe it or not, the snake did finally eat the pie. It sounds like a tall story but it's true, I can't account for it except that there might have been some savoury meat or something sticking to the pie.

Chapter 14

Herpetologists I have known

I wish I knew more herpetologists. Three, in particular, who interest me are: the Belgian, Dr Rollinat, whose high opinion of the intelligence of the sand lizard I have referred to; Dr Malcolm Smith, the authority on British reptiles; and Dr Karl Patterson Schmidt, whose experience in fieldwork throughout the world must have been unequalled. The three whom I know, or rather knew, for two of them are dead, are Norman Douglas, C. F. Ionides and Reginald Lanworn, still very much with us. One of my millionaire's day-dreams is of going on an expedition with those three. The career of Reginald Lanworn is enormously encouraging. Born in Cambridge-shire, he became an underkeeper at the Reptile House in Regent's Park Zoo when he was a youth. He could not afford higher educa-tion, though today he would have been given a grant and might be on his way towards a Chair of Zoology. By studious application he became so learned that the special post of Herpetologist was created for him.

When I first met Ionides on one of his very rare visits to England he was wearing khaki trousers, cricket-shirt, ancient brown sand-shoes, and his famous magic green hat, indescribably tattered and, I believe, venom-bespattered. He had been staying with his mother in Hove. On anyone else, this get-up for London might have seemed a bit affected, but although he certainly had a sense of showmanship, there was not a trace of affectation about him. He was entirely natural and all of a piece, so much so that you forgot what an odd piece he was.

We had lunch with Alan Wykes at the Savage Club and went on to Portland Place to do a sound radio broadcast. After the preliminary run-through, during which Ionides and I talked herpetology, the very young producer turned to me and said: 'That's exactly what I don't want.' Ionides looked at me and winked. When we went on the air we repeated our conversation almost word for word.

Ionides interested me very much and I took a great fancy to him. We talked snakes all the time, but I got the feeling that I knew him quite well, and everything I learned about him afterwards – the terrific beatings at Rugby, how on a singlehanded safari in India he hid for hours in a heap of elephant-dung, his hatred of missionaries, passion for history and violent heroes, savage outbursts at unsatisfactory Africans, total indifference to comfort – all fitted into place.

At first glance he might have seemed a wisp of a man, but you soon sensed his stringy toughness. He had a soft voice to match his sensitive shadowy face, and a laconic way of speaking. In spite of some deafness, due to a kick from an elephant, he was a good listener as well as a brilliant talker, and conversation with him was a genuine two-way exchange. No one, clothes apart, could have been more civilised, less farouche, yet there was something distinctly other-worldly about him. Margaret Lane, who has written vividly and movingly about him in her *Life with Ionides*, is right when she calls his profile 'notably satyric'. He had remarkable physical charm and I couldn't keep my eyes off him.

Constantine Ionides, known to his family and friends as Bobby and in Africa nicknamed, rather irritatingly, Iodine, came from a Greek merchant family that had been settled in England for 150 years. After Rugby and Sandhurst he was posted to the South Wales Borderers in India, then seconded to the King's African Rifles, arriving in 1925 in Tanganyika, where he was to spend most of his life. Two years later his report read: 'It would be to his advantage and that of the Service if this officer took as much interest in his profession as he does in big game hunting.' So he resigned his commission, did some elephant poaching and became for a time a white hunter. When his clients proved too unbearable, he would lead them right up to the buffalo's nose.

In 1933 he gave up poaching and joined the Tanganyika Game Department, first as Elephant Control Officer at £40 a month – he had a private income of £200 a year. Later he became a Game Ranger. Experiences during this period, including encounters with

maneaters, being mauled by an elephant, okapi-hunting with
pygmies, are told in interesting detail, but rather conventionally –
for Ionides was no great shakes as a writer – in his autobiography,
A Hunter's Story. What does emerge from this book, apart from
Ionides' prowess on safari and his analysis of the sensations of
fear, is his passionate interest in animals and his conversion from
hunter to naturalist.

His chief exploit in World War Two was rounding up some
Somalis who had been armed to cause trouble by the Italians. His
method was to capture all the best-looking Somali women, put them
behind barbed wire and let it be known that if the Somali men
wanted them back they must surrender their rifles.

Snake-catching, for which Ionides was best known in this country
through books about him by Alan Wykes and Margaret Lane, came
comparatively late in his life. He had always been fond of snakes
and had caught a few here and there. In India, as subaltern, he kept
a rat snake christened Sylvia after a girl friend (he never married,
thought marriage a trap, couldn't expect any woman to share his life,
which, when not nomadic – at one time he thought it unhealthy to
spend more than four days in one place – was phenomenally
uncomfortable).

In 1943 a museum curator asked him if he could supply him with
mambas, cobras and boomslanges for the Nairobi Snake Park. The
first notable capture was a black mamba, the largest and most
dangerous venomous snake in Africa. Ionides tackled it with too
short a forked stick, was very nearly bitten but just managed to grab
it behind the head. After this he evolved what he called the Ionides
snake-catcher, 'a sophisticated stick with a running noose attached to
the fork'.

For catching the green mamba, that beautiful tree-climbing snake,
he had a special grab-stick, designed with pincers at the end of a long
pole. He first tried it out on a big black mamba, a female who had
just killed two villagers. He brought her down from a low branch and
bagged her safely, although her head and 4 feet of body were rearing
up from the grab. His description of the lovely bloom on her freshly
cast skin is quite lyrical. (It is characteristic of herpetologists that they
tend to appreciate the beauty of venomous snakes more than that of

nonvenomous ones. When, on the outbreak of war in 1939, the king cobra at the London Zoo had to be decapitated by order of the Cabinet, tears were shed in the Reptile House.)

Green mambas climb high, and in his snake-catching prime, before the thrombosis in his legs that eventually killed him, Ionides used to go after them up to a height of 40 feet and more. He would get furious if anyone hinted there was anything lax about his safety precautions. These were, in fact, scrupulous, and anyone who went snake-hunting with him had complete confidence.

None the less, he was bitten thirteen times. Once was when he tried out the immunity recipe of an African who had survived the bite of a black mamba. Ionides chose a small night adder, poisonous but not normally deadly. He experienced no symptoms, so in case the snake might have exhausted its venom he gave it a night's rest and made it bite him again next morning.

All the other bites he put down to mistakes on his part. The worst was from a puff adder which he had been trying to tame. He was also spat at by a spitting cobra which he was catching without wearing goggles; he shut his eyes just in time and the venom ran down his cheeks. He used to handle the gaboon viper, a big thick viper with a marvellous skin like an Oriental rug and a copious supply of particularly deadly venom, almost as if it were a puppy. He knew what he was about for, by day at any rate, the sluggish gaboon viper is blessed with an angelic disposition. Also there is no question that Ionides had a special affinity with snakes. He approached them with a rhythmic deftness and vatic concentration.

After his retirement from the Game Service, in 1956, snake-catching became his main occupation. He supplied zoos and laboratories and had a highly organised system of snake scouts. He didn't make much money out of it, but it allowed him to live the bush life he loved, first at Ziwale, then based at a dusty bats'-urine-stained bungalow at Newala on the edge of a plateau near the Mozambique border. And it remained a persistent passion.

Margaret Lane tells how the news of snakes in the neighbourhood – it teemed with them – would galvanise him into feverish yet disciplined action. Towards the end of his life he became more and more apprehensive about the new Africa and the destruction of wildlife. He was a reactionary, but a mystical rather than a political one. Benevolence and savagery were strangely fused in him.

A minor herpetologist, whose unconventional dress and habitat would have appealed to Ionides, was Brusher Mills, a familiar figure in the New Forest. He caught adders and grass snakes and the oc-

Henry (Brusher) Mills, the
New Forest snake-catcher

casional smooth snake and sold them to animal dealers and the Reptile House of the Zoo. He lived in a hut in the forest near Brockenhurst. His Christian name was Harry, but he was known as Brusher because of the meticulous way in which he brushed the New Forest cricket pitch between innings. A large stone marks his grave in Brockenhurst churchyard with a carving of Brusher and his hut in the trees. His death was tragic. According to an old Forest law if a man lives on a piece of land for thirty years he has right to claim it as his own. Brusher Mills had lived in his hut for twenty-nine years and 364 days. He came home a few hours before sundown to find his hut had been burned to the ground. It broke his heart and he died soon afterwards on 1st July 1905, aged 67.

Chapter 15

Reptiles in Captivity

Nobody should keep any wild animal in captivity unless he can give it proper living conditions and is prepared to make some serious study of it. Most reptiles are unsuitable as pets; yet it is surprising how easy some are to look after — especially some species of snakes.

Presumably, for all except the dedicated herpetologist, the venomous species are simply not on. Only a criminal lunatic would recommend them. This does not mean to say some of them cannot be tamed and accustomed to being handled. Ionides could take liberties with poisonous snakes, but he was a law unto himself. And when catching wild snakes and caging them he always observed rigid security precautions.

Many a poisonous snake if handled gently, and above all calmly, with never a sudden movement, will lose its fear and aggression. This certainly applies to our British adder, *Vipera berus*. I have often caught adders by flicking them with the point of a stick out onto an open space. When the adder straightened out and began moving I picked it up carefully by the end of its tail between finger and thumb. This is safe enough so long as you hold it well away from your body, because the adder cannot lift its head high enough to bite your hand. (For heaven's sake don't try this on with one of the larger venomous snakes.)

From then on the process of taming can begin. One adder enthusiast I know used to go into raptures of anthropomorphism over what he insisted was the female adder's gentle smile. As a boy, I used to transport adders home in a wine bottle. You carefully lower the adder so that its head goes down the neck of the empty bottle. I was never allowed to keep one for more than a day. Just as well; adders do not do well in close confinement; they are nervous little snakes and refuse to feed. Curious, the fascination they have for the young herpetologist. Not so long ago a twelve-year-old boy was caught raiding the open-air vivarium at the London Zoo just inside the main entrance by the Monkey House. He had three adders in his pocket and confessed to two more at home. There were plenty of grass snakes and some fine green lizards, but his soul yearned only for adders. He should have a future.

I feel I may be in danger of misleading the young, so let me emphasise that it is never safe to handle *any* venomous snake, however expert you may think you are. If you are cautious and gentle enough you have a fair chance of not being bitten, but a fair chance is not good enough. There is always the danger that some sudden noise or movement over which you have no control may shatter the rapport you think you have established. Ionides was sitting one morning after breakfast in his dressing-gown, in his house in Tanzania, with a young puff adder on his lap. He thought he had it tamed and was stroking its head. A breeze sprang up. A curtain flapped. The puff adder snapped and caught Ionides in the finger, fortunately with one fang only; but it was quite a nasty little bite.

The rashness of some herpetologists is indeed extraordinary. They really do ask for it. Here is one instance from the history of the London Zoo's Reptile House quoted by Ramona and Desmond Morris in *Men and Snakes*, from *The Times* of 21st October 1852.

Edward Curling, aged 31, was brought to University College Hospital yesterday morning, October 20th. His occupation was that of a keeper at the Zoological Gardens, and the care of the Reptile House was his special duty. About 8 a.m., while engaged at his work in his department, he commenced a series of rash familiarities with some of the venomous serpents. After removing an African cobra from its cage, and twirling it about his head, he replaced it without having received any injury and took out an Indian cobra. This he also played with for some time with impunity, allowing it to crawl round his body beneath his waistcoat. Shortly afterwards, however, while he was holding the snake before his face the creature made a dart at him, and inflicted a wound on the upper part of his nose, etc. In forty minutes past 9 a.m. he was a corpse.

One of the most tragic deaths in the history of herpetology was that of Dr Karl Patterson Schmidt of the Chicago Natural History

Museum. I never met him, but I have made free use of his learning throughout this book. A few years ago a small specimen of the boomslange (*Dispholidus typus*) was sent to him for identification. It bit Schmidt while he was examining it. He died twenty-four hours later. With truly scientific stoicism he kept a detailed record of his symptoms, among them bleeding from the mouth, bladder and rectum. Death was actually caused by respiratory failure. One is reminded of Kipling's short story 'Rhinegelder and the German Flag' about a German herpetologist who was fatally bitten while taking a liberty with a multi-coloured snake which he thought was a harmless species. Kipling, no doubt, had heard of the confusion there used to be between the highly venomous American coral snakes, one of which is marked with black, red and yellow bands, and their non-venomous relations (see p. 91). But an expert herpetologist like Rhinegelder would certainly have known how to distinguish between a coral snake and a nonvenomous colubrine. I do not know the exact circumstances in which Dr Schmidt was bitten; no doubt it was one of those untoward accidents.

Anyone can spot a viper, but it is not easy to distinguish between many nonvenomous colubrines and venomous elapines; as for distinguishing between nonvenomous colubrines and venomous back-fanged *Boiginae*, this requires a highly experienced expert. One can imagine the predicament of a herpetologist with limited field experience who arrives for the first time in a tropical country where snakes are abundant. How far dare he rely on his book-learning and zoo and museum study? For the behaviour of many perfectly harmless snakes can be quite intimidating. . . .

I remember an Aesculapian snake which I caught in the Forest of Fontainebleau. This is excellent snake terrain, but I had had no luck for two days. Sometimes it is like that; you prowl around in what ought to be an ideal locale and nothing shows up. Then Juliette, the twelve-year-old daughter of Desmond Ryan, the friend with whom I was staying in the village of Recolles, said she would take me to a part of the forest nearby where I could be certain of a snake. She must have had a natural bent for ecology, for almost as soon as she waved her hand and said 'Anywhere round here' I spotted a brown snake curled up in a little scoop in a rock. I looked hard at it before

I picked it up to make quite sure it couldn't be a viper, because it was partly in the shade. I had no doubt at all that it was an Aesculapian, but it struck several times at the back of my hand, inflicting tiny teeth marks and drawing blood. I had a momentary pang of anxiety. Might it conceivably be a mutation? Have not some suggested that there is a tendency for colubrines to evolve towards venomous forms? Three seconds later Aesculapius settled down quietly in my hand.

Perhaps at this point, before considering harmless species like the Aesculapian, that really are more or less suitable as pets, I may digress into snake charming. This is a most fascinating subject, also rather a maddening one because it is difficult to separate fraud and showmanship and mumbo jumbo from fact.

Let us dispose of the more flagrant tricks that snake charmers have been getting up to since the time of Herodotus. In North Africa they have been faking the horned viper, *Cerastes cornutus*, by inserting artificial horns into the head via the mouth and telling you: 'See de snake dat bit de Queen of Egypt in de tit.' The snake charmers of North Africa, though some are said to have a rapport with their pets and treat them with respect, seem to be rather inferior to the Indian snake charmers. Cobras with their spectacular habit of rearing up 2 or 3 feet of their bodies and spreading their hoods are always the favourite performers and the North African cobra has not such a widespread hood as the Indian.

It used to be thought that the cobra's swaying in time to the snake charmer's pipe was just showmanship and the snake was following the snake charmer's movements. But although snakes are almost certainly both tone and tune deaf they are extremely sensitive to all vibrations and their forked tongues may act as accessory auditory organs. Another snake which Indian snake charmers sometimes carry around in their baskets is Russell's viper. This was the murderous pet of Dr Grimesby Roylott, the manic villain in Conan Doyle's story 'The Speckled Band'; it would have been quite incapable of climbing up the ventilator. The doctor should have tamed a mamba or possibly a hamadryad. My impression is that Sax Rohmer's Dr Fu Manchu was the better herpetologist.

Indian snake charmers practise several methods of rendering cobras harmless. They may draw the snake's fangs by making it bite a cloth which they then snatch away. They may clip them out with scissors or burn them out with a hot iron; sometimes they sew up the snake's mouth. But any reptile house keeper will tell you a snake's mouth is notoriously sensitive and injury is likely to cause necrosis of the bone. It seems unlikely that any of the brutal methods would commend themselves to an intelligent snake charmer. Drawing the fangs, however, need not be injurious if it is done carefully. Snakes in the wild shed their fangs repeatedly and have always a crop in reserve. Another less drastic technique is to milk the snake of its venom before the performance. Neither method is absolutely reliable because it is always possible for some venom to dribble down and get into a wound caused by an ordinary tooth; also it is difficult to milk a snake so that not a drop of venom remains.

Stories of special remedies such as the snake-stone, a piece of horn supposed to be porous and to absorb the venom, can be dismissed. But immunity by inoculation with the snake's saliva is a possibility. Sceptics, from Pliny and Galen onwards, would have you believe that all snake charmers work with snakes that have been made harmless. (Galen, incidentally, described another method: plugging the snake's fangs with wax.) It is difficult to check the evidence, but it does seem to be highly probable if not certain that some snake charmers work with snakes that have not been tampered with in any way, and the snake in whose case the evidence is most impressive is the most dangerous of all, the hamadryad or king cobra (see Chapter 8). The women of some of the hill regions of Burma make a ritual cult of the hamadryad,[1] approaching it with that ambivalent attitude of reverence and scorn often reserved for totem animals. They tease them, make them strike at them and miss and strike again; they even kiss the hamadryads on the top of their heads.

But there is no need to become mystical. Many snakes tame quickly after a few seconds of writhing about. Species and individuals

[1] The Snake Temple on the island of Penang is infested with swarms of *Trimeresurus wagleri*, an arboreal viper about 3 feet long, by no means unvenomous (see p. 108). It never bites the congregation. It has, however, a very sluggish disposition, is regarded as lucky, and natives in Borneo and Sumatra encourage it to settle near their huts.

vary very much, but in many cases if the snake is handled regularly it will not revert to the wild nervousness of the first few seconds after capture. This applies to venomous as well as nonvenomous snakes.

There is another factor which is sometimes forgotten and that is the tendency to exaggerate the speed of all snakes' movements. A rattlesnake's measured speed of striking is about 8 feet per second. This is far less than the speed of a boxer's punch. And a cobra striking from the up-reared position is slower than a rattlesnake. I have seen caged cobras striking at a cap dangled in front of them on a stick, and I was surprised how easy it was to make them miss by twitching the cap aside at the last moment. After missing there was an interval during which the snake had to pull its head back and rear up before striking again. This slowness accounts for the ease with which the sly mongoose defeats a cobra in a fight. I suppose it is conceivable that by making a cobra miss often enough you might establish a kind of negative conditioned reflex.

The only person I knew who claimed to have kept a cobra as a pet was the late Roy Campbell, the South African poet whose poem 'To a Pet Cobra' I have quoted in the anthology. I questioned him about this once, but it was late in the afternoon and he was very vague about details. I did not press him because he, too, had a habit of striking unexpectedly.

And now for the nonvenomous snakes. A small python or boa constrictor needs quite simple accommodation; so long as it is kept warm and dry, a plain wooden cage with a floor of newspaper or sand will do. You must make sure there is something for the snake to rub against when changing its skin.

Many a young Indian python or boa belonging to a stage performer, belly-dancer or stripteaser, has never known a proper cage, being carted round the globe in a canvas bag and exercised on the chair-backs in theatrical digs. And yet they seem to do well enough. There is no limit to the indignities to which an innocent snake will submit at the hands of a naked showgirl, allowing her to pop its head halfway down her throat, or between her legs, while she writhes about in a pseudo-erotic frenzy that inflames the audience of sales managers and their customers and goes down on the expense account

Boa constrictor (*Constrictor constrictor*). The commonest of the New World constrictors, ranging from Mexico to the Argentine. Has been known to reach eighteen feet but the average length is much less. Often a good captive.

as 'special entertainment for the overseas sales drive'. (A genuinely repulsive exhibition is that given by a Japanese cabaret artist, Miss Ongawa. She inserts the head of a living snake into her mouth and guides it so that the head emerges through one of her nostrils. I have no particular objection to this and I don't suppose the snake has either. What I do most vehemently disapprove of is that Miss Ongawa then proceeds to eat the snake alive.)

The lighter variety of the Indian python has a docile disposition and should be perfectly manageable up to a length of 8 feet. There was one in the Reptile House at the Zoo which my daughter wore round her neck when she was seven. The African royal python also has an excellent reputation. Young boa constrictors are favourites with stage performers. I had an unfortunate experience with a boa-constrictor in Harrods; he snapped at me like a bad-tempered poodle and gave me a quite painful though harmless bite on the hand. Perhaps he thought I was a shoplifter.

You must always be a bit careful about winding any really strong snake around your neck. Ditmars tells an alarming story about his friend, the artist Charles Higby, who kept several snakes in his New York studio. Most were boas and never gave him any trouble. One day he was given a fine large 8-foot-long specimen of the Florida pine snake, a colubrine, not a boa, but a powerful constrictor. It was in an atrocious temper when it arrived and hissed and struck at him repeatedly. When it had calmed down a little Higby set about taming it. He tipped it out of its cage on to a rug, gently lifted it and draped it round his neck. The snake seemed quite quiet, but a sudden movement disturbed it and it coiled tightly round his neck. When Higby tried to dislodge it, it contracted its coils so tight that he began to choke. He plucked at the coils but couldn't find the snake's head or tail with which to start unwinding. He was on the verge of losing consciousness, as the coils were squeezing his carotid artery and interrupting the blood supply to his brain. Then he had an inspiration; he staggered over to the looking-glass above the mantelpiece and located the tail poking up behind his ear.

Occasionally snake dancers have a little trouble with their partners. One night in 1944 in a posh Hollywood nightclub a girl who was doing a turn with a python got into a bit of difficulty. The python appeared to resent her treading on his tail; anyway he struck at her savagely. Rescue came not from any Tarzan or his understudy, but from the nonagenarian Lady Mendl's octogenarian miniature poodle, Mr Bluey. Leaping down from his mistress's lap he dashed at the python, bit it in the neck and worried it – in spite of his having only two teeth which met – so severely that it retreated under a table.

The problem of diet is not so difficult, because most snakes feed at intervals. A young python or boa should make do with a rat once a fortnight. It might eat a pigeon. You might be able to get it to take lumps of raw beef. The food should be fairly fresh-killed. Snakes are always attracted by movement and one tame snake could be induced to seize a sausage dressed up in a mouse's skin and twitched about realistically by its owner with a string.

If a snake refuses dead food the process of feeding it live food is not so atrocious as you might think. If the snake is hungry it makes one quick strike at its prey, throws several coils round it and squeezes it to death in a very few seconds. If it isn't hungry it won't take the slightest notice of it, and neither will the prey, if it is a rat or a mouse, take the slightest notice of the snake. I have seen a mouse which had been introduced too early into the cage of an Aesculapian snake sitting on the snake's head eating crumbs with every appearance of enjoyment; for once the condemned man really did make a hearty breakfast. (Mice, incidentally, have been known to go for adders and bite them in the head.)

If you decide to keep snakes in a vivarium remember that all snakes or lizards coming from tropical countries need artificial heat in cold climates. The temperature should not be allowed to go below 70° F.

For European and North American snakes from temperate zones the vivarium should be reasonably spacious, with a layer of dry soil or sand. There must be branches for climbing, the higher the better, and something for these very secretive creatures to hide under; a broken flower pot will do. Also there must be a bowl of drinking water. Most snakes like swimming and the best way of satisfying their aquatic need is to take them out of the cage and give them a swim in the bath.

The grass snake is the only English species suitable for captivity, and its habits have already been described. Of European snakes, one of the most suitable is the four-lined snake (see p. 170). It tames easily and feeds well and readily on mice, lizards and eggs. It is an active climbing snake and needs plenty of space.

The Aesculapian snake has also been described. Opinions vary about its disposition. My own experiences with it have been most harmonious. I kept one for some months in a London flat and it never showed any sign of ill-temper and seemed to like being handled. It spent a lot of time climbing about a wheel-back armchair at which I sat working. It thrived on one mouse every ten days. Its excreta seemed to consist of little else but the pelt. Its climbing feats were remarkable. There was a small hole in one wall of the sitting-room about 8 feet from the floor where a gas pipe went in. One afternoon I looked up from my writing and saw the tail of the snake disappearing into the hole. The climb was quite perpendicular and it must have been difficult to get any purchase between pipe and wall. I caught hold of the tail and pulled very carefully and steadily. At first the snake resisted and I was afraid of injuring it, but I managed to haul it out unhurt except for a chipped ventral scale. It showed no resentment. Was the hole associated with mice? Or was there any kind of conscious attempt at escape? Another time it was missing for two days and then discovered underneath the mattress of a bed – a reversion to hibernation perhaps.

Less suitable is the leopard snake (*Elaphe situla*) found in southern Italy, the Balkans, several Mediterranean islands, Turkey and the Caucasus. Its habits are much the same as those of the Aesculapian. This is perhaps the most beautiful snake in Europe, with large ver-milion spots ringed with black on a beige background. I kept one for a short time and though it let itself be handled it never became really tame. Every time I put down my hand to pick it up it made a little half-hearted strike at me. It looked as if it was in good condition, but I felt it was too nervous to settle down and feed.

Of the North American snakes, the several species of garter snakes are easy to keep. The bull snake, a voracious mouse-eater, also does well in captivity. The various species of colubrines known as racers, of which there are several examples in America and a few in Europe, make unhappy prisoners and are better left free. One North American snake that does well in captivity is the indigo snake. Also suitable is the handsome king snake. It must be kept by itself, as it is a cannibal. It can swallow and digest snakes a good deal longer than itself. This is illustrated by an amazing X-ray photograph in Ditmars' *Snakes of the World*.

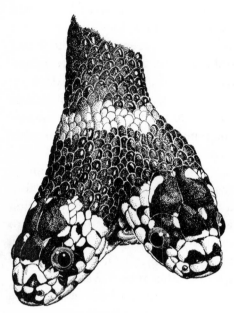

Two-headed Californian king snake
(Lampropeltis gelulus)

The phenomenon of two-headedness is not uncommon in snakes, particularly in king snakes and garter snakes. Each head is alive and will take food. There was one two-headed garter snake at the New York Zoo in which each head had a little more neck than is usual in these cases. The two heads had to be separated by a little cardboard collar to prevent them biting each other.

Everyone who decides to keep a snake should remember that there is still an enormous amount to be found out and that he can, provided he makes exact observations, regard himself as a potential research worker. Patience will almost certainly lead to some discovery. No one, as far as I know, has written a paper on 'Types of individual behaviour met with among grass snakes (or garter snakes) in captivity'. There is no reason why a snake should not be approached as an individual so long as one is careful not to fall into the bog of anthropomorphism. For anyone living in a tropical country there are all sorts of possibilities. One that occurs to me, though I dare say work may have already been done on it, is an ecological study of snakes in relation to man; snakes that haunt farms or peasant slums because of the plentiful supply of rats. . . .

Lizards are so much more mobile than snakes that I can't help having doubts about the suitability of most species for close confinement.

I have described in Chapter 3 the splendid European eyed or jewelled lizard. It does quite well in captivity, I think, but if it is to be a prisoner it should be given roomy quarters, preferably an open-air vivarium in a sheltered place with a southern aspect. Incidentally, the conditions in which reptiles are kept in many animal dealers' shops are disgraceful.

One of the more refined pleasures of herpetology is catching, taming and admiring at close quarters, and then releasing. It is best enjoyed in a terrain where the reptile life is fairly profuse. I remember one delightful day just before the start of World War Two, at the Pont du Gard near Nîmes. Wall lizards and common lizards[1] were swarming over the huge stones at the base of the Roman aqueduct. A few yards away by the river's bank I caught a tessellated water-snake, played with it for a while, then set it free; it obliged me by taking a header into the river and I watched it swim away under water. A little further on I flushed a fine pair of green lizards. The one I chased made it easy for me by running up a sapling. He didn't know what to do when he got to the top; I picked him off, tamed him and took him for a drink at the café on the other side of the aqueduct before releasing him.

The ideal relationship with lizards is only possible in a southern country where, if you find the right spot, they may come and feed at your table while retaining complete independence, as Norman Douglas describes in *Alone*.

Of English lizards the common lizard does well in an open-air or

[1] The late A. L. Lyall told me he once saw a barrow-load of tortoises in Kensington with the notice: USEFUL PETS: KILLS INCESTS AND OTHER PESTS.

closed vivarium on a diet of flies and mealworms. *Anguis fragilis*, the slow-worm, has been known to live to the age of fifty-six. The beautiful and, now anyway, relatively rare sand lizard (*Lacerta agilis*) is apt to dwindle and die in captivity. It is better to release it if you are lucky enough to catch one.

Of American lizards some of the *Anolis* genus do well enough, though they would need artificial heat in an English climate.

I have described in Chapter 5 the chamaeleon, and touched on its short span of life. My friend Mr R. D. Lanworn, who was the herpetologist at the London Zoo until his retirement in 1968, was tireless in his devotion to his charges and had – he still has – an expert eye for detail. He told me he had never succeeded in keeping a chamaeleon alive for more than two years. I think he remained sceptical of reports that chamaeleons have bred in captivity in this country.

My own experience was sad. In the autumn of 1966 I bought a fine specimen of an East African chamaeleon, about 10 inches long, and transferred it to an artificially heated cage which Mr Lanworn inspected and approved. The temperature was kept at 73° F. The chamaeleon was provided with a regular supply of flies and blue-bottles. For a time it seemed to be doing quite well. It clambered slowly and dreamily among the branches in its cage, shooting flies with its tongue. We treated it with the greatest care and respect, refraining from sexing it lest the examination proved traumatic. We named it Tiresias after the legendary seer who lived both as a man and a woman. My daughter, Celia, spent a lot of time looking after it. We were delighted when she took it for a walk round a warm room on her arm and it shot down a November fly sitting on a curtain at a range of 8 inches. Mr Lanworn had been pessimistic from the start, although he had no fault to find with its conditions. He warned us that we should be lucky if we got Tiresias to live through the winter. He was only too right. Gradually the chamaeleon went off its food and began to dwindle in front of our eyes. It gave up climbing and lay on the floor of the cage. One morning we found it dead. When I took it out there was so little flesh on its body that it might have been a hollow paper toy.

I was too disheartened to try again. Could it have been an old specimen nearing its natural end? Mr Lanworn did not think so. Solitary confinement? He thought that if anything chamaeleons did better in solitary than two or more up in a cell. Other chamaeleon-fanciers, of course, have had better luck. David Attenborough, I know, regards Mr Lanworn, for all his superior expertise, as unduly pessimistic.

If you must keep a tropical lizard in captivity you will probably do better with a South American iguana. These need a large cage with plenty of branches for climbing and, of course, artificial heating from a light bulb. Their diet is a simpler matter because of their being partly vegetarian, but they are apt to suffer from vitamin deficiency and rickets if kept to an exclusively non-protein diet.

Never, of course, put lizards in the same cage as snakes.

And never miss an opportunity of inspecting a shop that sells reptiles, however unpromising it may look. You do not know what you may find. Once in London, before the war, in a little temporary dump off the Haymarket, they were selling up the stock of some bankrupt travelling circus. There was a box of stumpy Australian skinks which stank to heaven when I poked my nose in. Next door to them was a pair of the most beautiful lizards I have seen. About 14 inches long and, to the best of my recollection, an exquisite dark sapphire blue. The little man in charge of them had no idea where they came from except that it was somewhere in the East Indies. I think they may have been a species of agamid found in Sumatra. He was asking fifty shillings for the pair, a bargain even then, but I was going abroad the next day. When I came back the shop was gone.

Some of the crocodilians make rather more suitable pets than you might expect, especially young American alligators. They eat meat readily and splash about in a warm bath. There was a craze for baby alligators in America at one time and it was rumoured that unscrupulous dealers were selling the young of the large South American species. Perhaps it was this that gave rise to the myth which circulated at cocktail parties that giant alligators were prowling the sewers of New York – the adult forms of baby alligators which had been accidentally flushed down lavatory pans. A howling lie of course, but typical of the fantasies which reptiles attract.

Some of the largest crocodilians become very docile in captivity, and live for a long time. One crocodile in the Jardin des Plantes in Paris, named *l'homme qui rit,* was alleged to have been kept there for eighty-three years. In the Reptile House at the London Zoo there used to be a huge American alligator about 15 feet long named George. The late Mr Budd, to whom I talked in 1950 when he was then the Head Keeper, told me that during the war when the cares of the world were weighing heavily upon him he used to go into George's cage of an evening after closing time and sit on his back and smoke a pipe. After a few minutes' silent communion with the venerable descendant of the archosaurs he felt a lot better.

It was Budd who told me the sad story of 'Bloody Sunday' in the Reptile House, 3rd September 1939, the day war was declared. The Chamberlain Government, magnificently unprepared in nearly every other respect, had taken counsel with Sir Julian Huxley, then Secretary of the Zoological Society, and it had been arranged that the moment the first air-raid siren sounded all poisonous snakes were to be decapitated lest the idea of their escaping might cause a panic in North London. The measure may sound extreme, but there was sense in it, particularly during that fine summer weather. The cobras, with which the house was then well stocked, might have made for the drains and caused not only panic but perhaps a few fatalities. In winter they would have died in a few hours. So, when the siren (a false alarm) sounded just after Chamberlain had finished speaking the Reptile House staff set about their task of mass liquidation. 'It was sickening', said Budd. 'There we were, choppin' away hour after hour, choppin' the heads off thousands of pounds' worth of valuable venomous reptile.' Mr Lanworn, who confirmed the story, told me he was not ashamed of shedding a tear over the headless corpse of the prize specimen, that magnificent female hamadryad 16 feet 9 inches long.

Some of the chelonians make interesting pets, but only land tortoises are suitable for cold climates. The two species you find in English gardens[1] are *Testudo graeca* and *Testudo marginata.* Both will do well if properly looked after and are easy to feed on greenstuff, lettuce and fruit. But thousands die each year from neglect. If they

[1] An interesting subject would be a comparison between members of this ubiquitous species taken from different countries.

are caught out in a sudden frost they are done for. It is better not to let them wander at large in a garden, but to keep them in a sunny enclosure, making sure they have proper winter quarters for hibernation. They have, as we have remarked, a reputation for intelligence, and are well worth studying. Famous English historical tortoises include Archbishop Laud's which was kept, on a long string through a hole in its shell, in his garden at Lambeth Palace. It lived according to varying reports for either 80 or 107 years, and died because a stupid gardener dug it up for a bet and omitted to put it back in its hibernating place. There was also the tortoise of Peterborough which has been credited with ages from 92 to 220 years.

Here, by way of a brief recap, is a little table of suitable reptiles that can be kept in captivity:

LIZARDS

Species	Diet	Quarters
European green lizard	Mealworms, flies and worms plus a little raw meat	Open-air vivarium in summer, or dry cage with plenty of space, bracken, heather, and water always available
Common lizard	Same as above	Same as above
Eyed lizard	Same as above	Same as above
Slow-worm	Small insects and slugs	Same as above

In climates such as Britain's all the above should be kept indoors except during summer months, but do not need artificial heat.

The following lizards are quite suitable for captivity, but if they are to be kept in northern climates their cages should be artificially heated by an electric light bulb and the temperature should not be allowed to drop below 70°:

Species	Diet	Quarters
Common iguana	Fruit and especially bananas, dandelion flowers and some raw meat, as iguanas may occasionally eat meat and may suffer in captivity from vitamin deficiency	The cage should be roomy with plenty of branches for the iguana to climb on. Water always available
Other iguanas and iguanids	All other iguanids (with the exception of the black iguana of South America and the crested iguana of the Galapagos Islands) are non-vegetarian and feed on insects and spiders and small mammals. In captivity they should be given chopped meat	
Anolis	Non-vegetarian. Same as above diet	Spacious cage with branches for climbing

SNAKES

Species	Diet	Quarters
Grass snake	Frogs and tadpoles. Also yolk of eggs	The cage should be roomy with branches for climbing. It should be kept dry, but a pan of water should be supplied and some cover
Aesculapian snake	One mouse every ten days should suffice. Raw meat and yolk of egg may be offered	Same as above

SNAKES (*contd*)

Species	Diet	Quarters
Four-line snake	Same as above	Same as above
Garter snake	Earthworms, frogs, mice. Try also raw meat and yolk of egg	Same as above

None of the above need artificial heat in their quarters but in temperate climates except during summer months should be kept indoors.

Indigo snake	Mice, and rats for large specimens. Raw meat yolk of egg	Extra spacious with branches as this is a large active snake. The temperature of the cage should not be allowed to fall below 65° F
Boa constrictor	Same as above	Same as above
Pythons of suitable species, e.g. young Indian pythons and	Rats or rabbits or pigeons according to size of snake	Same as above
African royal pythons	Same as above	Same as above

ALLIGATORS

Species	Diet	Quarters
American alligator	Raw meat and eggs	A 'swimming' bath should be available. but part of the cage should be kept dry. Cage temperature minimum 65°

The care of suitable tortoises and terrapins has already been described.

An Anthology of
Reptilian Belles-lettres

This anthology consists of poems and prose extracts. The poetry starts with Virgil's description of the great snake that coiled round Anchises' tomb (*Aeneid* V) and the extraordinary episode in the story of Cadmus in Ovid's *Metamorphoses* when Cadmus, in old age, is talking to his wife and wonders whether that serpent could have been a sacred one which was transfixed by his spear when he set out from Sidon and scattered the snake's teeth over the ground to be the seeds of new men. After a prayer to the gods he metamorphoses into a snake and his wife does the same.

The herpetological observation in both these passages is quite accurate. Dr Karl Schmidt suggests that Virgil had probably seen an African python in captivity in Rome. Ovid, I feel quite convinced, had witnessed snakes courting and copulating. No doubt he gave them his blessing.

The extract from Gower's *Confessio Amantis* is a delightful little piece of mythical moralising. The other poems, which are all printed complete, range from the seventeenth century to D. H. Lawrence and some of the moderns. All the four Orders are represented, as the tuatara (Order *Rhynchocephalia*) is mentioned by Marianne Moore.

The prose extracts include some obvious and inevitable choices such as the ever-delightful Gilbert White of Selborne and Norman Douglas on snakes and lizards from *Alone*, which is my favourite of his books, and a charming piece from Colette. The anecdote from the Rev. J. G. Wood's *Natural History* is typically Victorian. Readers will already have made the acquaintance of Dipsas, the perfectly harmless thirst-snake which struck such terror into Lucan.

In the introduction I have touched on the serpent myth and the

Fall. The extract from Ramona and Desmond Morris's entrancing *Men and Snakes* makes an interesting pendant.

There is a characteristically racy description of water-moccasin hunting by the late Raymond L. Ditmars, who has been so many readers' first introduction to herpetology.

I have myself condensed, with the author's permission, James Stern's 'The Man Who Was Loved' and added the extraordinary hitherto unwritten sequel which he told me over the telephone. I have called it 'The Story of a Snake Story'.

The Aeneid
Virgil

dixerat haec, adytis cum lubricus anguis ab inis
septem ingens gyros, septens volumin traxit,
amplexus placide tumulum lapsusque per aras,
caerulese cui terga notae maculosus et auro
squamam incendebat fulgor, ceu nubibus arcus
mille iacit varios adverso sole colores.
obstipuit visu Aeneas. Ille agmine longo
trandem inter pateras et levia pocula serpens
libavitque dapes, rursusque innoxius imo
successit tumulo, et depasta altaria liquit.

Ended he had, when from the temple's base,
A slippery serpent, of gigantic size,
Trailed forth seven circles coiling seven times round
And gently clasped the tomb, and glided o'er
The altars; azure-marked the back of him
And gleam of spots of gold lit up his scales;
As when within the clouds the bow that fronts
The sun flings forth a thousand varied hues.
Awestricken at the sight Aeneas stood;
He, twining in his marshalled length at last
Twixt the meats, and then again withdrew
Harmless within the basement of the tomb;
And left the altars he had fed upon.

Aeneid, Book V, lines 84–93. English rendering
by T. H. Delabere May

Metamorphoses
Ovid

Iamque malis annisque graves dum prima retractant
Fata domus releguntque suos sermone labores,
'Num sacer ille mea traiectus cuspide serpens'
Cadmus ait 'fuerat, tum cum Sidone profectus
Vipereos sparsi per humum, nova semina, dentes?
Quem si cura deum tam certa vindicat ira,
Ipse precor serpens in longam porrigar alvum'.
Dixit, et ut serpens in langam tenditur alvum
Durataeque cuti squamas increscere sentit
Nigraque caeruleis variari corpora guttis
In pectusque cadit pronus, commissaque in unum
Paulatim tereti tenuantur acumine crura.
Bracchia iam restant; quae restant bracchia tendit
Et lacrimis per adhuc humana fluentibus ora
'Accede, o coniunx, accede miserrima' dixit,
'Dumque aliquid superest de me, me tange manumque
Accipe, dum manus est, dum non totum occupat anguis'.
Ille quidem vult plura loqui, sed lingua repente
In partes est fissa duas, nec verba volenti
Sufficiunt, quotiensque aliquos parat edere questus,
Sibilat: hanc illi vocem natura reliquit.
Nuda manu feriens exclamat pectora coniunx:
'Cadme, mane teque, infelix, his exue monstris!
Cadme, quid hoc? Ubi pes, ubi sunt umerique manusque
Et color et facies et, dum loquor, omnia? Cur non
Me quoque, caelestes, in eandem vertitis anguem?'
Dixerat; ille suae lambebat coniugis ora
Inque sinus caros, veluti cognosceret, ibat
Et dabat amplexus adsuetaque colla petebat.
Quisquis adest (aderant comites), terrentur; at illa
Lubrica permulcet cristati colla draconis,
Et subito duo sunt iunctoque volumine serpunt,

Donec in appositi nemoris subiere latebras.
Nunc quoque nec fugiunt hominem nec vulnere laedunt
Quidque prius fuerint, placidi meminere dracones.

Now Cadmus and his wife, burdened with old age and its afflictions, were recalling all the early misfortunes of their family and reminding each other of them. 'I wonder,' said Cadmus, 'whether it could have been a sacred snake, that one I stabbed with my spear the time I set out from Sidon, and sowed its teeth to raise a crop of men? If it was, and if the Gods are avenging it on me so fiercely, may I be stretched out and elongated into a snake myself.' As he spoke he did indeed begin to be extended into a long snake-form. His skin became tough and scales grew on it and his body turned black and speckled with blue spots. He lay down on his belly and his legs were joined together and drawn out into a pointed tail. His arms were still there, however, and he held them out to his wife and the tears ran down his still human face. 'Come here', he said, 'and touch me while there is still something of me left, and hold my hand while it is still a hand before the snake absorbs me utterly.' He would have liked to have said more but his tongue was becoming forked; he could not utter words but began to hiss. His wife struck her bare breast with her hand. At first she railed at him for his monstrous serpent shape. 'Where are your feet and hands, your face and shoulders?' Then she called out on the gods to change her too into a snake. Cadmus, all snake now, licked her face with his forked tongue and made for her loving arms and coiled round her neck. Some who were there besides the two were terrified, but the wife of Cadmus was unafraid. She stroked the ser-pent]s neck. And suddenly there were two snakes and they writhed together with their coils entwined. Then they went off into the cover of a neighbouring wood. After that they did not harm men neither did they flee from them, but behaved like tame dragons, remember-ing what they once had been.

Metamorphoses, Book IV, lines 569–603

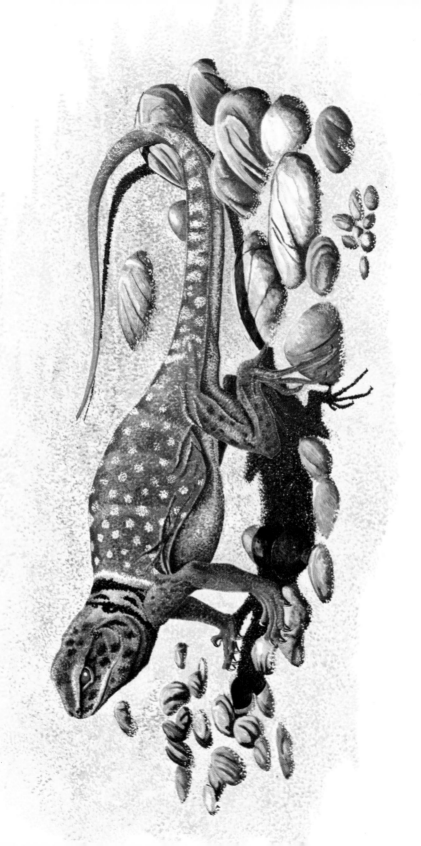

Eastern collared lizard (*Crotaphytus collaris collaris*). This handsome North American Iguanid is an active terrestrial species with a fine, long cylindrical tail. Its minatory posture reminds one rather of its African cousins, the Agamids.

John Gower

There is a serpent, Aspidis
By name, whose property is this:
The carbuncle, which people call
The noblest gem-stone of them all,
It wears high up within its head;
And when a cunning man is led
To want the stone and tame the snake
By singing cantrips he will make,
When Aspidis begins to hear,
He lies down flat upon his ear,
Close to the ground, and stops it tight;
The other ear, with all his might
He closes with his tail — so well
That not a word of all the spell,
That should enchant him, stirs his sense;
Such is the serpent's self-defence,
By means of which he turns away
Words that might lead his ear astray.

Confessio Amantis, lines 463–83. Modern
English rendering by Terence Tiller

On the Crocodile
Thomas Heyrick

I
I am the Terrour of the Sea,
Proud *Nile's* chief Glory and his Fear:
From far I dart upon my Prey,
Which to my watry Hold I bear.
Dogs dare not drink for doubt of Me,
Tho they 'gainst Bulls and Lyons dare.
I am chief Instrument of Fate;
Two Elements upon me wait;
Water and *Land* conspire to make me great.

II
Of food I no Distinction make,
But in my Cruelty am Just;
Of Man and Beast alike I take,
And eat them both with equal Gust.
With Draughts of Gore my thirst I slake,
And Flesh I down my throat do thrust.
Fear gave rise to Divinity;
And Gods have rose from Cruelty:
Wise *Aegypt* showd so; when she worship'd me.

III
The *Indians* kill me for their Food,
And say, I am Delicious meat;
They drink of their Relation's Blood,
And eat, what did their Fathers eat.
In me they injure their own Brood,
Their Malice doth their Judgement cheat.
But I may yet a Question make,

Whether when Me they hunt and take,
They think their Hunger or Revenge to slake.

IV

No Creature can my *Power* withstand:
Yet to that power *Deceit* I tie:
And by this Double *Gordian* band
Secure my hungry Tyranny;
The Terrour of the Sea and Land
In ambush on the Sands I lie.
What e're I take I do devour,
Yet o're the Head I tears do shower,
And weep and grieve, — because I have no more.

V

Men me Abhor, yet Imitate;
Like Falsehood use without all Shame:
As Lawless Power, as deep Deceit
Doth *Christian under Christian* tame:
I live i' th' Actions of the Great;
What they're to Others, to them I am.
Would you then Power and Cunning see
Mixed with deep Hypocrisie?
They are conjoyn'd in *Man*, as well as *Me*!

A Crocodile
Thomas Lovell Beddoes

Hard by the lilied Nile I saw
A duskish river-dragon stretched along,
The brown habergeon of his limbs enamelled
With sanguine alamandines and rainy pearl:
And on his back there lay a young one sleeping,
No bigger than a mouse; with eyes like beads,
And a small fragment of its speckled egg
Remaining on its harmless, pulpy snout;
A thing to laugh at, as it gaped to catch
The baulking merry flies. In the iron jaws
Of the great devil-beast, like a pale soul
Fluttering rocky hell, lightsomely flew
A snowy trochilus, with roseate beak
Tearing the hairy leeches from his throat.

A Narrow Fellow
Emily Dickinson

A narrow fellow in the grass
Occasionally rides;
You may have met him, — did you not?
His notice sudden is.

The grass divides as with a comb,
A spotted shaft is seen;
And then it closes at your feet
And opens further on.

He likes a boggy acre,
A floor too cool for corn.
Yet when a child, and barefoot,
I more than once, at morn,

Have passed, I thought, a whip-lash
Unbraiding in the sun, —
When, stooping to secure it,
It wrinkled, and was gone.

Several of nature's people
I know, and they know me;
I feel for them a transport
Of cordiality;

But never met this fellow,
Attended or alone,
Without a tighter breathing,
And zero at the bone.

Snake
D. H. Lawrence

A snake came to my water-trough,
On a hot, hot day, and I in pyjamas for the heat,
To drink there.

In the deep, strange-scented shade of the great dark carob-tree
I came down the steps with my pitcher
And must wait, must stand and wait, for there he was at the trough
    before me.

He reached down from a fissure in the earth-wall in the gloom
And trailed his yellow-brown slackness soft-bellied down, over the
    edge of the stone trough
And rested his throat upon the stone bottom,
And where the water had dripped from the tap, in a small clearness,
He sipped with his straight mouth,
Softly drank through his straight gums, into his slack long body,
Silently.

Someone was before me at my water-trough,
And I, like a second comer, waiting.

He lifted his head from his drinking, as cattle do,
And looked at me vaguely, as drinking cattle do,
And flickered his two-forked tongue from his lips, and mused a
    moment,
And stooped and drank a little more,
Being earth-brown, earth-golden from the burning bowels of the
    earth
On the day of Sicilian July, with Etna smoking.

The voice of my education said to me
He must be killed,
For in Sicily the black, black snakes are innocent, the gold are
    venomous.

And voices in me said, If you were a man
You would take a stick and break him now, and finish him off.

But I must confess how I liked him,
How glad I was he had come like a guest in quiet, to drink at my
    water-trough
And depart peaceful, pacified, and thankless,
Into the burning bowels of this earth.

Was it cowardice, that I dared not kill him?
Was it perversity, that I longed to talk to him?
Was it humility, to feel so honoured?
I felt so honoured.

And yet those voices:
If you were not afraid, you would kill him!

And truly I was afraid, I was most afraid,
But even so, honoured still more
That he should seek my hospitality
From out the dark door of the secret earth.

He drank enough
And lifted his head, dreamily, as one who has drunken,
And flickered his tongue like a forked night on the air, so black,
Seeming to lick his lips,
And looked around like a god, unseeing, into the air,
And slowly turned his head,
And slowly, very slowly, as if thrice adream,
Proceeded to draw his slow length curving round
And climb again the broken bank of my wall-face.

And as he put his head into that dreadful hole,
And as he slowly drew up, snake-easing his shoulders, and entered
    farther,
A sort of horror, a sort of protest against his withdrawing into that
    horrid black hole,

Deliberately going into the blackness, and slowly drawing himself
      after,
Overcame me now his back was turned.

I looked round, I put down my pitcher,
I picked up a clumsy log
And threw it at the water-trough with a clatter.

I think it did not hit him,
But suddenly that part of him that was left behind convulsed in
      undignified haste,
Writhed like lightning, and was gone
Into the black hole, the earth-lipped fissure in the wall-front,
At which, in the intense still noon, I stared with fascination.

And immediately I regretted it.
I thought how paltry, how vulgar, what a mean act!
I despised myself and the voices of my accursed human education.
And I thought of the albatross,
And I wished he would come back, my snake.

For he seemed to me again like a king,
Like a king in exile, uncrowned in the underworld,
Now due to be crowned again.

And so, I missed my chance with one of the lords
Of life.
And I have something to expiate;
A pettiness.

Baby Tortoise
D. H. Lawrence

You know what it is to be born alone,
Baby tortoise!

The first day to heave your feet little by little from the shell,
Not yet awake,
And remain lapsed on earth,
Not quite alive.

A tiny, fragile, half-animate bean.
To open your tiny beak-mouth, that looks as if it would never
    open,
Like some iron door;
To lift the upper hawk-beak from the lower base
And reach your skinny little neck
And take your first bite at some dim bit of herbage,
Alone, small insect,
Tiny bright-eye,
Slow one.
To take your first solitary bite
And move on your slow, solitary hunt.
Your bright, dark little eye,
Your eye of a dark disturbed night
Under its slow lid, tiny baby tortoise,
So indomitable.

No one ever heard you complain.

You draw your head forward, slowly, from your little wimple
And set forward, slow-dragging, on your four-pinned toes,
Rowing slowly forward.
Whither away, small bird?

Rather like a baby working its limbs,
Except that you make slow, ageless progress
And a baby makes none.

The touch of sun excites you,
And the long ages, and the lingering chill
Make you pause to yawn,
Opening your impervious mouth,
Suddenly beak-shaped, and very wide, like some suddenly gaping
     pincers;

Soft red tongue, and hard thin gums,
Then close the wedge of your little mountain front,
Your face, baby tortoise.

Do you wonder at the world, as slowly you turn your head in its
     wimple
And look with laconic, black eyes?
Or is sleep coming over you again,
The non-life?

You are so hard to wake.

Are you able to wonder?
Or is it your indomitable will and pride of the first life
Looking round
And slowly pitching itself against the inertia
Which had seemed invincible?

The vast inanimate,
And the fine brilliance of your so tiny eye,
Challenger.

Nay, tiny shell-bird,
What a huge vast inanimate it is, that you must row against,
What an incalculable inertia.

Challenger,
Little Ulysses, fore-runner,
No bigger than my thumb-nail,
Buon viaggio.

All animate creation on your shoulder,
Set forth, little Titan, under your battle-shield.
The ponderous, preponderate,
Inanimate universe;
And you are slowly moving, pioneer, you alone.

How vivid your travelling seems now, in the troubled sunshine,
Stoic, Ulyssean atom;
Suddenly hasty, reckless, on high toes.

Voiceless little bird,
Resting your head half out of your wimple
In the slow dignity of your eternal pause.
Alone, with no sense of being alone,
And hence six times more solitary;
Fulfilled of the slow passion of pitching through immemorial ages,
Your little round house in the midst of chaos.

Over the garden earth,
Small bird,
Over the edge of all things.

Traveller,
With your tail tucked a little on one side
Like a gentleman in a long-skirted coat.

All life carried on your shoulder,
Invincible fore-runner.

Lizard
D. H. Lawrence

A lizard ran out on a rock and looked up, listening
no doubt to the sounding of the spheres.
And what a dandy fellow! the right toss of a chin for you
and swirl of a tail!

If men were as much men as lizards are lizards
they'd be worth looking at.

From Lamia
John Keats

The God, dove-footed, glided silently
Round bush and tree, soft-brushing, in his speed,
The taller grasses and full-flowering weed,
Until he found a palpitating snake,
Bright, and cirque-couchant in a dusky brake.

She was a gordian shape of dazzling hue,
Vermilion-spotted, golden, green, and blue;
Striped like a zebra, freckled like a pard,
Eyed like a peacock, and all crimson barred;
And full of silver moons, that, as she breathed,
Dissolved, or brighter shone, or interwreathed
Their lustres with the gloomier tapestries —
So rainbow-sided, touched with miseries,
She seemed, at once, some penanced lady elf,
Some demon's mistress, or the demon's self.
Upon her crest she wore a wannish fire
Sprinkled with stars, like Ariadne's tiar:

Her head was serpent, but ah, bitter-sweet!
She had a woman's mouth with all its pearls complete:
But weep, and weep, that they were born so fair?
As Prosperine still weeps for her Sicilian air.
Her throat was serpent, but the words she spake
Came, as through bubbling honey, for Love's sake,
And thus; while Hermes on his pinions lay,
Like a stooped falcon ere he takes his prey.

To a Pet Cobra
Roy Campbell

With breath indrawn and every nerve alert,
As at the brink of some profound abyss,
I love on my bare arm, capricious flirt,
To feel the chilly and incisive kiss
Of your lithe tongue that forks its swift caress
Between the folded slumber of your fangs,
And half reveals the nacreous recess
Where death upon those dainty hinges hangs.

Our lonely lives in every chance agreeing,
It is no common friendship that you bring,
It was the desert starved us into being,
The hate of men that sharpened us to sting:
Sired by starvation, suckled by neglect,
Hate was the surly tutor of our youth:
I too can hiss the hair of men erect
Because my lips are venomous with truth.

Where the hard rock is barren, scorched the spring,
Shrivelled the grass, and the hot wind of death
Hornets the crag with whirred metallic wing –
We drew the fatal secret of our breath:
By whirlwinds bugled forth, whose funnelled suction
Scrolls the spun sand into a golden spire,
Our spirits leaped, hosannas of destruction
Like desert lilies forked with tongues of fire.

Dainty one, deadly one, whose folds are panthered
With stars, my slender Kalihari flower,
Whose lips with fangs are delicately anthered,
Whose coils are volted with electric power,
I love to think how men of my dull nation

Might spurn your sleep with inadvertent heel
To kindle up the lithe retaliation
And caper to the slash of sudden steel.

There is no sea so wide, no waste so sterile
But holds a rapture for the sons of strife:
There shines upon the topmost peak of peril
A throne for spirits that abound in life:
There is no joy like theirs who fight alone,
Whom lust or gluttony have never tied,
Who in their purity have built a throne,
And in their solitude a tower of pride.

I wish my life, O suave and silent sphinx,
Might flow like yours in some such strenuous line,
My days the scales, my years the bony links,
The chain the length of its resilient spine:
And when at last the moment comes to strike,
Such venom give my hilted fangs the power,
Like drilling roots the dirty soil that spike,
To sting these rotted wastes into a flower.

A Dying Viper
Michael Field

The lethargy of evil in her eyes –
As blue snow is the substance of a mere
Where the dead waters of a glacier drear
Stand open and behold – a viper lies.

Brooding upon her hatreds: dying thus
Wounded and broken, helpless with her fangs,
She dies of her sealed curse, yea, of her pangs
At God's first ban that made her infamous.

Yet, by that old curse frozen in her wreath,
She, like a star, hath central gravity
That draws and fascinates the soul to death;

While round her stark and terrible repose,
Vaults for its hour a glittering sapphire fly,
Mocking the charm of death. O God, it knows!

To My Tortoise Ananke
Eugene Lee-Hamilton

Say it were true that thou outliv'st us all,
   O footstool once of Venus; come, renew
Thy tale of old Greek isles, where thy youth grew
In myrtle shadow, near her temple wall;

Or tell me how the eagle let thee fall
   Upon the Greek bard's head from heaven's blue,
   And Apathy killed Song. And is it true
That thy domed shell would bear a huge stone ball?

O Tortoise, Tortoise, there are weights, alack!
   Heavier than stone, and viewless as the air,
Which none have ever tried upon thy back;

Which, ever and anon, we men must bear —
   Weights which would make thy solid cover crack
And how we bear them, let those ask who care.

The Plumet Basilisk
Marianne Moore

IN COSTA RICA

In blazing driftwood
    the green keeps showing at the same place;
as, intermittently, the fire-opal shows blue and green.
    In Costa Rica the true Chinese lizard face
is found, of the amphibious falling dragon, the living fire-work.

He leaps and meets his
    likeness in the stream and, king with king,
helped by his three-part plume along the back, runs on two
    legs,
tail dragging; faints upon the air; then with a spring
dives to the stream-bed, hiding as the chieftain with gold
    body hid in

Gutavita Lake,
    He runs, he flies, he swims, to get to
his basilica — 'the ruler of Rivers, Lakes, and Seas,
    invisible or visible', with clouds to do
as bid — and can be 'long or short, and also coarse or fine at
    pleasure'.

THE MALAY DRAGON

We have ours; and they
    have theirs. Ours has a skin feather crest;
theirs has wings out from the waist which is snuff-brown or
        sallow.
Ours falls from trees on water; theirs is the smallest

dragon that knows how to dive head-first from a tree-top to
    something dry.
Floating on spread ribs,
    the boat-like body settles on the
clamshell-tinted spray spring from the nutmeg-tree —
    minute legs
    trailing half akimbo — the true divinity
of Malay. Among unfragrant orchids, on the unnutritious
    nut-

tree, *myristica*
    fragrans, the harmless god spreads ribs that
do not raise a hood. This is the serpent-dove peculiar
    to the East; that lives as the butterfly or bat
can, in a brood, conferring wings on what it grasps, as the
    air-plant does.

THE TUATARA

Elsewhere, sea lizards —
    congregated so there is not room
to step, with tails laid criss-cross, alligator-style, among
    birds toddling in and out — are innocent of whom
they neighbour. Bird-reptile social life is pleasing. The Tuatara
will tolerate a
    petrel in its den, and lays ten eggs
or nine — the number laid by dragons since 'a true dragon
    has nine sons'. The frilled lizard, the kind with no legs,
and the three-horned chameleon, are non-serious ones that
    take no flight

if you do not. In
    Copenhagen the principal door
of the bourse is roofed by two pairs of dragons standing on
    their heads — twirled by the architect — so that the four

green tails conspiring upright, symbolise four-fold security.
  Now,

where sapotans drop
    their nuts out on the stream, there is, as
I have said, one of the quickest lizards in the world – the
    basilisk – that feeds on leaves and berries and has
shade from palm-vines, ferns, and peperonias; or lie bask-
        ing on a

horizontal branch
    from which sour-grass and orchids sprout. If
best, he lets go, smites the water, and runs on it – a thing
    difficult for fingered feet. But when captured – stiff
and somewhat heavy, like fresh putty on the hand – he is no
        longer

the slight lizard that
    can stand in a receding flattened
S-small, long and vertically serpentine or, sagging,
    span the bushes in a fox's bridge. Vines suspend
the weight of something's shadow fixed on silk. By the
    Chinese brush, eight green

bands are painted on
    the tail as piano keys are barred
by five black stripes across the white. This octave of faulty
    decorum hides the extraordinary lizard
till night-fall, which is for man the basilisk whose look will
    kill; but is

for lizards men can
    kill, the welcome dark – with the galloped
ground-bass of the military drum, the squeak of bag-pipes
    and of bats. Hollow whistled monkey-notes disrupt
the castanets. Taps from the back of the bow sound off on
    last year's gourd,

or when they touch the
   kettledrums – at which, for there's no light,
a scared frog screaming like a bird, leaps out from weeds in
     which
   it could have hid, with curves of the meteorite,
   wide water-bug strokes,
in jerks which express
a regal and excellent awkwardness,

   the plumet portrays
mythology's wish
to be interchangeably man and fish –

travelling rapidly upward, as
spider-clawed fingers can twang the
bass strings of the harp, and with steps
as articulate, make their way
back to retirement of strings that
vibrate till the claws are spread flat.

   Among tightened wires,
minute noises swell
and change as in the wood's acoustic shell

   they will, with trees as
avenues of steel
to veil invisibleness ears must feel –

black opal emerald opal
emerald – the prompt-delayed loud-
low chromatic listened-for-down-
scale which Swinburne called in prose, the
noiseless music that hangs about
the serpent when it stirs or springs.

No anonymous
   nightingale sings in a swamp, fed on

sound from porcupine-quilled palm-trees blurring at the
    edge, that
rattle like the rain. This is our Tower-of-London
jewel that the Spaniards failed to see, among the feather
    capes and hawk's-

head moths and black-chinned
    humming-birds; the innocent, rare, gold-
defending dragon that as you look begins to be a
    nervous naked sword on little feet, with three-fold
separate flame above the hilt, inhabiting fringe equidistant

from itself, of white
    fire eating into air. Thus nested
in the phosphorescent alligator that copies each
digression of the shape, he pants and settles — head
up and eyes black as the molested bird's, with look of
    whetted fierceness,

in what is merely
    breathing and recoiling from the hand.
Thinking himself hid among the yet unfound jade axe-
    heads,
    silver jaguars and bats, and amethysts and
polished iron, gold in a ten-ton chain, and pearls the size of
    pigeon-eggs,

he is alive there
    in his basilisk cocoon beneath
the one of living green; his quicksilver ferocity
    quenched in the rustle of his fall into the sheath
which is the shattering sudden splash that marks his
    temporary loss.

The Snakes
Colette

Four days ago these two poor, shy creatures were dragged away from the banks of their pool with its cool reeds, and from the warm knoll whose grey and tawny earth, crackling under the sun, their own colours imitate. They had an abominable journey, crammed into a case with two hundred of their fellows, all jumbled up together and rustling; and the dealer who chose me these two was continually stirring up this living skein of gleaming ropes, and disentangling with his energetic fingers their pale bellies and mottled backs, some of them thin as boot-laces and others tough as whips.

'That one's a male,' he said, 'and that's a big female. They won't be so bored if you take the two.'

I have no means of knowing whether it is boredom that makes them stretch themselves out along the window-panes of their cage. When I first had them, in their fear they banged the walls of their prison so hard that I nearly let them loose in the garden. One of them struck the same spot, where two panes join, unceasingly with his hard little nose; the other shot up in a single spring to the wire-netting of the roof, fell back limp as a steel rod about to melt, and began all over again. It was tempting to offer them both their freedom in the garden, with its lawn and the holes in the wall, But the fierce, gay she-cats were on the watch, ready to claw those vulnerable scales and scratch out those bright, gold eyes.

So I kept the snakes and in them, once again, I pity the wretched wisdom of wild creatures who resign themselves to captivity although they never abandon the hope of regaining their freedom. If I bend for a long time over my snakes, the hidden western horror of the reptile revives in me and I understand how one can become stupefied with the spectacle of their obstinate dance, of that endless word which they write against the window-pane, and with the mysterious movement of a body which advances without limbs, alternately reabsorbing itself and protruding beyond itself.

But the evil spell vanishes as soon as I touch the snakes and take hold of them. Dry, smooth and cold, they are rebellious to the touch, and there is something pleasurable in playing with their strength. The male, who is the thinner of the two, darts his agile head, with its little black and yellow cap, and the cunning flame of his tongue, in all directions. He writhes and knots his long body, its belly inlaid with blue, silver and greenish white, about my arm, and then unrolls himself, carefully testing the warmth of my hand with his chin and throat; and while he lingers there, undecided, I can feel his cold little heart throbbing in my palm.

With the other hand I hold back the solid female, round whom my fingers scarcely meet. She is in a bad temper, lashing out with her tail and head and hissing like a gander, and I know not how to soothe the harmless anger of this creature who, by some oversight, was created weaponless. A burning ray of sunshine falls on my lap, just what I wanted to lay the snakes there. After some moments of silent struggle, they lie quite still there in the warmth; then all at once, like a stubborn resilient spring suddenly yielding, they relax, in a way that makes me hope I have not so much conquered them as charmed them.

There they lie on my knees, motionless but alert. One of them, gripping the arm of my chair with its tail, lets its head hang down to the edge of my skirt, feeling the air and the stuff with the ends of its quivering tongue. The other, coiled up like a limp rope, allows me for the time being to raise its body and guide it with my hand as if it were a piece of braid trimming; but at the slightest movement of the bitch lying a few feet away, it shudders and grows taut. No matter, for the first time we have established a truce, the snakes and I; and even in the uncertain calm of this first hour we can contemplate those that are to come. Already it seems to me that they have become more human, and they, for their part, believe that I am growing tamer.

From **Life with Ionides**
Margaret Lane

In the old days Ionides used to go up the trees himself, but his lame-
ness prevents him now and he is not sorry; he has a poor head for
heights. Instead he waits at the bottom with his grab-stick, head
thrown back, shading his eyes with his hand; his sharpness of vision
is as good as ever, and he gives occasional directions to the climber,
who by this time may be lost in a maze of leaves.

At the first mamba-catching I saw there were two snakes, coiled
together in the topmost plateau of leaves perhaps fifty feet from the
ground, and there was a ripple of laughter when a black arm was
thrown up to point and a woman cried out gleefully that they were
making love. Certainly they seemed unaware of danger; their coils
were wreathed together like a garland, and the leaves moved slightly
in a way that was different from the gentle stir of the breeze.
Rashidi, the senior snake-hand, who climbs (or so it seemed to me)
only when there is a particularly good audience, murmured something to Pétu, who sought about on the bole of the tree for a grip,
and with the serious and modest air which never leaves him began
methodically to climb. He went always barefoot in the early days of
my visit (for a reason which had nothing to do with climbing and
which I was to discover later) and his black legs and feet went
steadily up the smooth limbs until he had reached a point of rest
where he could pause and look down, stretching out his hand for the
top of the long grab being softly passed up to him. This is a hollow
metal tube fifteen feet along, with hinged claws at the top which are
opened and closed by a lever at the lower end, and which can be
locked by a screw. It is not unlike a pruning implement, except that
the cusps, instead of meeting together like scissors on a cutting edge,
are smooth, and close on the body of the snake more like a handcuff
on a wrist, uncomfortably tight, perhaps, but hardly painful.

He now climbed further out of sight, trailing the grab after him
and searching for a secure fork into which he could wedge his body,
and for a branch on which the heavy pole could be rested while he

passed it cautiously up in the right direction. The snakes seemed still unconscious, and since Pétu had now climbed so high as to be almost invisible except for the pallid blur of his ragged shorts, I came out into the sun and stood at a little distance, from which I could detect the ring of green which was not leaves, swaying with halcyon calm in its lofty cradle. Suddenly there was a glint of metal as the jaws of the grab closed over a looped coil, and a whip-lash of green flung out from the top of the tree, the long body casting and coiling, but held fast. A small head appeared momentarily out of the leaves, turn- ing on a slender neck to take stock of the thing that so inexplicably held it, and then withdrew abruptly to the foliage, which rippled with its tentative efforts to follow its mate. But the metal jaws, which had caught it a little behind the middle of the body, held fast and were not to be eluded, and it tried first one direction and then another, gliding off at speed among the leaves and curving back in dismay a moment after, staring in fierce astonishment at the trap.

Ionides and Rashidi were now beside me, holding up their grabs like lances in the air, waiting for the moment when Pétu could lower the snake within their reach. It was difficult to disentangle from the tree, coiling its long tail among the branches, winding like a tendril round handfuls of leaves and twigs, desperately seeking a hold, a balance, any purchase which might give leverage and set it free. But it was thrust out at last, and appeared suddenly against the sky, looping and winding about the pole like the caduceus of the ancients, the rod of Hermes, and was tilted slowly outwards and finally down. The waiting grabs were ready with open jaws; as soon as the snake was within reach they closed upon it, a careful distance apart; the metal grab was released on a word of command and the living knot, like a trophy proudly borne on the points of spears, came down to be laid at length on the dusty ground.

Here at last the beautiful creature could be seen at close quarters, no longer freely moving with an effortless ripple, threading like a ribbon of green through the spangled tree, but humbled by the metal cuffs locked on its body, writhing in the grip of an enemy it would never comprehend. But it was not defeated. It reared up as far as it could and struck at the trap, attacking the hard metal with smooth jaws, so that venon ran down and trickled in drops on the sand.

When Ionides approached it turned and faced him, its smooth green head, so curiously, with its full dark eye, like the head of a bird, and measured the distance, waiting for the unknown enemy to come within range. He crouched before it, slowly advancing the tongs as though hypnotised, the gaze of man and snake intent on the point at which one would suddenly dart and the other evade, both warily watching and measuring, avid for the strike. The tongs struck first, and missed; like a flash the head had eluded the thrust and was poised afresh, neck arched and eyes unwavering; a thread of tongue flickered nervously in and out. Ionides moved closer and struck again, and this time the snake was caught at the end of the tongs, its bright head flattened and distorted under pressure, the eyes covered, the forked tongue protruding, grains of sand and dirt dribbling from the lips. No further movement was possible; the body was trapped in two places and the head compressed; only the end of the tail, the few inches not wrapped tightly around the shafts, continued to flail about for a fresh hold, whipping little marks and grooves in the soft dust.

Ionides held the tongs in one hand and groped behind him with the other. Rashidi was ready with a calico bag which he put over it like a glove, and the muffled hand came forward to take a careful grip round the neck of the snake. The tongs were discarded, and the snake's head, which a moment before I had thought irretrievably damaged, at once resumed its bird-like shape; the tongue flickered, the delicate pale jaws were slightly open, and the eyes, dark and intent as ever, still kept their unblinking watch on the chance of escape. I had been wrong in supposing that the head had suffered; the bones of the skull are supple, the skin elastic, and Ionides knows to a nicety what pressure to exert. He is concerned only to control the head and keep the mouth closed while he gets his hand on the neck in a safe grip; once that is achieved the snake is powerless to bite, and need never feel the grabs or tongs again. Before the holds are released, however, the snake must be sexed, and while the head is held firmly by hand the grabs are kept locked, and an assistant must grasp the thrashing tail and turn the vent upwards, massaging vigorously with a thumb until the sexual organs, powerless even in this humiliating posture to resist the stimulus of friction, moistly emerge from a neat aperture and reveal the sex of the captive for the written record.

Having watched Rashidi and Pétu a number of times I was soon allowed to perform this office myself, and had my first experience of handling a wild snake. The feeling is quite unlike one's expectation, the first touch conveying surprised pleasure, since the body is smooth and warm and urgently alive, so that contact with one's palm is reassuring, a pleasurable shock like physical recognition. But the snake is not reassured, and the little vent, held tight in its ring of protective muscle, witholds its secret; at first my thumb was too timid and considerate and the whip-like tail wound tightly around my wrist in a grip of protest. 'Harder,' said Ionides, 'rub harder,' and I indelicately pressed and urged with a circular motion until the lips of the aperture relaxed and a bud-like structure appeared and then another, as though one had been squeezing the secret organs of a plant. At the same time a bright orange fluid sprayed out and ran over my hand, vivid and granular, like liquid pollen, and Ionides was pointing to two little jutting protuberances, slanting stiffly away from each other in a sideways direction, and asking if I could see the two penises. I had not known there would be two, and relaxed my pressure in surprise, upon which the curious manifestation vanished like magic, the vent contracted, and the smooth underbody of the snake was as neat, as polished, as secretive as before. 'I'm sorry it's defecated on your hand,' said Ionides in a matter-of-fact voice, 'but don't relax your grip. You've got to roll the body up and get it in the bag.' (The pollen-coloured fluid, I afterwards found, had a faintly spicy smell like curry powder, perfectly inoffensive.) . . .

The taking of gaboon vipers went on day after day with great regularity, until one almost lost the sense of its being dramatic. Occasionally the snake would stir and show annoyance, swelling up its heavy body with an appearance of anger and giving a prolonged hiss as it deflated, but only one that I saw made any serious attempt to get away, pouring its length majestically over the leaves, the ribs rowing rhythmically under the patterned skin at is moved ponderously off in search of cover. But the mambas were very different. They were alert, sharp-sighted and super-brilliant green and sun-dazzle of the leaves, to re-appear magically in another inaccessible outpost of the tree, swan-neck raised above emerald coils, elegant head turned intently after the pursuer, whom they follow with the rapt gaze of a cunning bird. They love the brilliant foliage of the huge mango trees, which in sunlight exactly matches their own green, and lie all day in the warmth of the topmost branches, swaying in the wind, coiled like a silken rope and almost invisible.

The Natural History of Selborne
Gilbert White

8 OCTOBER 1770

A land tortoise, which has been kept for thirty years in a little walled court belonging to the house where I now am visiting, retires under ground about the middle of November, and comes forth again about the middle of April. When it first appears in the spring it discovers very little inclination towards food; but in the height of summer grows voracious; and then as the summer declines its appetite declines; so that for the last six weeks in autumn it hardly eats at all. Milky plants, such as lettuces, dandelions, sowthistles, are its favourite dish. In a neighbouring village one was kept till by tradition it was supposed to a hundred years old. An instance of vast longevity in such a poor reptile!

From Letter VII

12 APRIL 1772

While I was in Sussex last autumn my residence was at the village near Lewes, from whence I had formerly the pleasure of writing to you. On the 1st November I remarked that the old tortoise, formerly mentioned, began first to dig the ground in order to the forming its hybernaculum, which it had fixed on just beside a great tuft of hepaticas. It scrapes out the ground with its forefeet, and throws it up over its back with its hind; but the motion of its legs is ridiculously slow, little exceeding the hour-hand of a clock; and suitable to the composure of an animal said to be a whole month in performing one feat of copulation. Nothing can be more assiduous than this creature night and day in scooping the earth, and forcing its great body into the cavity; but, as the noons of that season proved unusually warm and sunny, it was continually interrupted, and called forth by the heat in the middle of the day; and though I continued there till the 13th November, yet the work remained unfinished. Harsher weather, and frosty mornings, would have quickened its operations. No part of its behaviour ever struck me more than the extreme timidity it always expressed with regard to rain; for though it has a shell that would secure it against the wheel of a loaded cart, yet it does discover as much solicitude about rain as a lady dressed in all her best attire, shuffling away on the first sprinklings, and running its head up in a corner. If attended to, it becomes an excellent weather-glass; for as sure as it walks elate, and as it were on tiptoe, feeding with great earnestness in a morning, so sure will it rain before night. It is totally a diurnal animal, and never pretends to stir after it becomes dark. The tortoise, like other reptiles, has an arbitrary stomach as well as lungs; and can refrain from eating as well as breathing for a great part of the year. When first awakened it eats nothing; nor again in the autumn before it retires: through the height of the summer it feeds voraciously, devouring all the food that comes in its way. I was much taken with its sagacity in discerning those that do it kind offices; for, as soon as the good old lady comes in sight who has waited on it for more than thirty years, it hobbles towards its benefactress with awkward alacrity; but remains inattentive to strangers. Thus not only 'the ox knoweth his owner, and the ass his master's crib', but the most abject reptile and torpid of beings distinguishes the hand that feeds it, and is touched with the feelings of gratitude!

P.S. – In about three days after I left Sussex the tortoise retired into the ground under the hepatica.

Letter XIII

30 AUGUST 1769

When I wrote to you last year on reptiles, I wish I had not forgot to mention the faculty that snakes have of stinking *se defendo*. I knew a gentleman who kept a tame snake, which was in its person as sweet as any animal while in good humour and unalarmed; but as soon as a stranger, or a dog or cat, came in, it fell to hissing, and filled the room with such nauseous effluvia as rendered it hardly supportable.

Thus the squnck, or stonck, of Ray's *Synop Quadr.* is an innocuous and sweet animal; but, when pressed hard by dogs and men, it can eject such a most pestilent and fetid smell and excrement, that nothing can be more horrible.

From Letter XXV

SELBORNE   29 APRIL 1776

On August 4th, 1775, we surprised a large viper, which seemed very heavy and bloated, as it lay in the grass basking in the sun. When we came to cut it up, we found that the abdomen was crowded with young, fifteen in number; the shortest of which measured full seven inches, and were about the size of full-grown earthworms. This little fry issued into the world with the true viper-spirit about them, show-ing great alertness as soon as disengaged from the belly of the dam: they twisted and wriggled about, and set themselves up, and gaped very wide when touched with a stick, showing manifest tokens of menace and defiance, though as yet they had no manner of fangs that we could find, even with the help of our glasses.

To a thinking mind, nothing is more wonderful than that early instinct which impresses young animals with a notion of the situation of their natural weapons, and of using them properly in their own defence, even before those weapons subsist or are formed. Thus a young cock will spar at his adversary before his spurs are grown; and a calf or a lamb will push with their heads before their horns are sprouted. In the same manner did these young adders attempt to bite before their fangs were in being. The dam however was furn-ished with very formidable ones, which we lifted up (for they fold down when not used) and cut them off with the point of our scissors. There was little room to suppose that this brood had ever been in the open air before; and that they were taken in for refuge, at the mouth of the dam, when she perceived that danger was approaching, because then probably we should have found them somewhere in the neck, and not in the abdomen.

From Letter XXXI

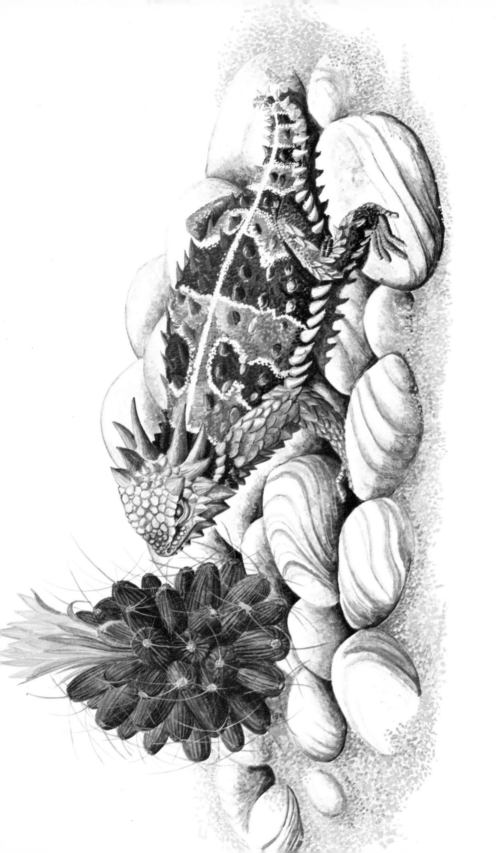

Texas horned lizard (*Phrynosoma cornutum*). Erroneously and all too often called the horned toad, this desert-dwelling North American Iguanid has the strange ability to squirt drops of bloods from its eyes when frightened.

SELBORNE 18 JUNE 1768

Providence has been so indulgent to us as to allow of but one venomous reptile of the serpent kind in these kingdoms, and that is the viper. As you propose the good of mankind to be an object of your publications, you will not omit to mention common salad-oil as a sovereign remedy against the bite of the viper. As to the blind worm (*Anguis fragilis*, so-called because it snaps in sunder with a small blow), I have found, on examination, that it is perfectly innocuous. A neighbouring yeoman (to whom I am indebted for some good hints) killed and opened a female viper about the 27th May; he found her filled with a chain of eleven eggs, about the size of those of a blackbird; but none of them were advanced so far towards a state of maturity as to contain any rudiments of young. Though they are oviparous, yet they are viviparous also, hatching their young within their bellies, and then bringing them forth. Whereas snakes lay chains of eggs every summer in my melon beds, in spite of all that my people can do to prevent them; which eggs do not hatch till the spring following, as I have often experienced. Several intelligent folks assure me that they have seen the viper open her mouth and admit her helpless young down her throat on sudden surprises, just as the female opossum does her brood into the pouch under her belly, upon the like emergencies; and yet the London viper-catchers insist on it, to Mr Barrington, that no such thing ever happens. The serpent kind eat, I believe, but once in a year; or rather, but only just at one season of the year. Country people talk much of a water-snake, but, I am pretty sure, without any reason; for the common snake (*Coluber natrix*) delights much to sport in the water, perhaps with a view to procure frogs and other food.

I cannot well guess how you are to make out your twelve species of reptiles, unless it be by the various species, or rather varieties, of our *Lacerti*, of which Ray enumerates five. I have not had opportunity of ascertaining these; but remember well to have seen, formerly, several beautiful green *Lacerti* on the sunny sandbanks near Farnham, in Surrey; and Ray admits there are such in Ireland.

From Letter XVII

SELBORNE   2 JANUARY 1769

It is a satisfaction to me to find that a green lizard has actually been procured for you in Devonshire; because it corroborates my discovery, which I made many years ago, of the same sort, on a sunny sandbank near Farnham in Surrey. I am well acquainted with the South Hams of Devonshire; and can suppose that district, from its southerly situation, to be a proper habitation for such animals in their best colours.

From Letter XXII

SELBORNE   28 FEBRUARY 1769

It is not improbable that the Guernsey lizard and our green lizards may be specifically the same; all that I know is, that, when some years ago many Guernsey lizards were turned loose in Pembroke College garden, in the University of Oxford, they lived a great while, and seemed to enjoy themselves very well, but never bred. Whether this circumstance will prove anything either way I shall not pretend to say.

From Letter XXIII

SELBORNE   21 APRIL 1780

The old Sussex tortoise, that I have mentioned to you so often, is become my property. I dug it out of its winter dormitory in March last, when it was enough awakened to express its resentments by hissing; and, packing it in a box with earth, carried it eighty miles in post-chaises. The rattle and hurry of the journey so perfectly roused it that, when I turned it out on a border, it walked twice down to the bottom of my garden; however, in the evening, the weather being cold, it buried itself in the loose mould, and continues still concealed.

As it will be under my eye, I shall now have an opportunity of enlarging my observations on its mode of life, and propensities; and perceive already that, towards the time of coming forth, it opens a breathing place in the ground near its head, requiring, I conclude, a freer respiration as it becomes more alive. This creature not only goes under the earth from the middle of November to the middle of April, but sleeps great part of the summer; for it goes to bed in the longest days at four in the afternoon, and often does not stir in the morning till late. Besides, it retires to rest for every shower; and does not move at all in wet days.

Whe one reflects on the state of this strange being, it is a matter of wonder to find that Providence should bestow such a profusion of days, such a seeming waste of longevity, on a reptile that appears to relish it so little as to squander more than two-thirds of its existence in a joyless stupor, and be lost to all sensation for months together in the profoundest of slumbers.

While I was writing this letter, a moist and warm afternoon, with the thermometer at 50, brought forth troops of shell-snails; and, at the same juncture, the tortoise heaved up the mould and put out its head, and walked about till four in the afternoon. This was a curious coincidence! a very amusing occurrence! to see such a similarity of feelings between the two φερέοικοι, for so the Greeks called both the shell-snail and the tortoise.

Summer birds are, this cold and backward spring, unusually late; I have seen but one swallow yet. This conformity with the weather convinces me more and more that they sleep in the winter.

More particulars respecting the old family tortoise

Because we call this creature an abject reptile, we are too apt to undervalue his abilities, and depreciate his powers of instinct. Yet he is, as Mr Pope says of his lord,

. . . Much too wise to walk into a well;

and has so much discernment as not to fall down a haha, but to stop, and withdraw from the brink with the readiest precaution.

Though he loves warm weather he avoids the hot sun; because his thick shell, when once heated, would, as the poets says of solid armour, 'scald with safety'. He therefore spends the more sultry hours under the umbrella of a large cabbage-leaf, or amidst the waving forests of an asparagus bed.

But, as he avoids heat in the summer, so, in the decline of the year, he improves the faint autumnal beams by getting within the reflection of a fruit-wall; and, though he never has read that planes inclining to the horizon receive a greater share of warmth, he inclines his shell, by tilting it against the wall, to collect and admit every feeble ray.

Pitiable seems the condition of this poor embarrassed reptile; to be cased in a suit of ponderous armour, which he cannot lay aside; to be imprisoned, as it were, within his own shell, must preclude, we should suppose, all activity and disposition for enterprise. Yet there is a season of the year (usually the beginning of June) when his exertions are remarkable. He then walks on tiptoe, and is stirring by five in the morning; and, traversing the garden, examines every wicket and interstice in the fences, through which he will escape if possible; and often has eluded the care of the gardener, and wandered to some distant field. The motives that impel him to undertake these rambles seem to be of the amorous kind; his fancy then becomes intent on sexual attachments, which transport him beyond his usual gravity, and induce him to forget for a time his ordinary solemn deportment.

Letter L

From **Reptiles of the World**
R. L. Ditmars

Sunning its heavy folds on a gnarled and twisted tree that rises from the coffee-coloured waters is a huge Moccasin. As our unwieldy craft glides toward it a sinister head turns in our direction, the jaws open widely, disclosing the white mouth-parts, while the outlines of a wicked pair of fangs show through their sheaths. Carefully manipulating the pole, we bring the 'boat' to a stop and advance the snake-noose on a long rod of bamboo. There is a quivering flash of the forked tongue and the reptile, preferring security to combat, slides with the ease of flowing oil down the twisted branches and into the water with such smoothness of motion that no splash accompanies its disappearance. A few bubbles mark the dive and we turn to stare at one another in mutual disappointment.

We had been snake-hunting through the bayous for half the day and several dozen harmless captives filled the bags. Relieving the guide from the tiresome punting of the flat-bottomed craft, the writer had posted his faithful and enthusiastic companion on the bow as look out as we spied this, our first cotton-mouth. But a little more than a week before the writer had left the North in a whirl of snow for a short stay in the wonderfully balmy air of the far Southern coast. From blustering winds and leafless trees to an atmosphere like the Northern June, the stately palmettoes and the live oaks with their garlands of hanging moss was a delicious change. Reptile life flourished in variety and plenty.

'That snake's an old timer and the boss of this swamp,' said the guide. 'There's not a copper-belly or a brown water snake in the bayou. He's cleaned them all out.'

As we floated into the bayou we played the rays of the swivel lamp upon the various sections of derelict timber in an endeavour to locate the low, gnarled tree we were in search of. A few seconds passed, with our hearts beating rapidly, when we beheld this on our left – and vacant. Speechless with disappointment, my guide involuntarily swung the lamp to the right, then raised its beam in what seemed a futile examination of the place.

'Hey,' he almost shouted. 'There he is.'

And sure enough, stretched in undulating fashion on the trunk of a fallen tree, lay the big 'cotton-mouth'. Huge he looked in the light of our lamp, his sides showing olive green, while the rough scales of the back seemed as black as velvet. Slowly turning toward the boat, he gave us a glassy stare and a flash of forked tongue. It was easy work slipping a noose over that wicked head, when we swung him, writhing furiously, into the boat. As my assistant, 'Charley' Snyder, turned the light inward and upon that struggling snake, the latter's villainy formed a scene that lingered long afterward with us all. Knotting and twisting about the pole, straining and contorting into uncanny shapes, jaws yawning and disclosing a pair of fangs that dribbled with the deadly yellow fluid as they rasped against everything in their reach, the picture spelled caution for us.

It was a job to thrill as we released the noose, and avoiding the well-aimed thrusts of the triangular head finally pinned that member to the floor of the craft with the heavy end of the snake-pole, when the creature was grasped by the neck. With Snyder holding open a large bag, the writer dropped the serpent within.

The Converted Snake
(A Hindu Legend)

A snake dwelt in a certain place. No one dared to pass by that way; for whoever did so was instantaneously bitten to death. Once a Mahatma [high-souled one] passed by that road, and the serpent ran after the sage in order to bite him. But when the snake approached the holy man he lost all his ferocity and was overpowered by the gentleness of the Yogin. Seeing the snake, the sage said: 'Well, friend, thinkest thou to bite me?' The snake was abashed and made no reply. At this the sage said: 'Hearken, friend; do not injure anybody in the future.' The snake bowed and nodded assent. The sage went on his way, and the snake entered his hole, and thenceforward began to live a life of innocence and purity without even attempting to harm any one. In a few days all the neighbourhood began to think that the snake had lost all his venom and was no more dangerous, and so every one began to tease him. Some pelted·him; others dragged him mercilessly by the tail, and in this way there was no end to his troubles. Fortunately the sage again passed by that way and, seeing the bruised and battered condition of the good snake, was very much moved, and inquired the cause of his distress. At this the snake replied: 'Holy Sir, this is because I do not injure any one after your advice. But alas! they are so merciless!' The sage smilingly said: 'My dear friend, I simply advised you not to bite any creature, still you should keep every one at a considerable distance by hissing at him.'

Similarly, if thou livest in the world, make thyself feared and respected. Do not injure any one, but be not at the same time injured by others.

From **The Illustrated Natural History**
Rev. J. G. Wood

The name Dipsas is derived from a Greek word, signifying thirst, and is given to this snake because the ancients believed that it was eternally drinking water and eternally thirsty, and that to allay in some degree the raging drought, it lay coiled in the scanty springs that rendered the desert passable. As they considered almost all Serpents to be venomous, and according to the custom of human nature, feared most the creatures of which they knew least, they fancied that the waters were poisoned by the presence of this dreaded Snake. Lucan, in the *Pharsalia*, alludes to this idea:

> And now with fiercer heat the desert glows,
> And mid-day gleamings aggravate their woes ;
> When lo ! a spring amid the sandy plain
> Shows its clear mouth to cheer the fainting train,
> But round the guarded brink, in thick array
> Dire aspics rolled their congregated way,
> And thirsting in the midst the horrid Dipsas lay.
> Blank horror seized their veins, and at the view,
> > Back from the fount the troops recoiling flew.

The ancient writers also averred that the bite of the Dipsas inoculated the sufferer with its own insatiate thirst, so that the victim either died miserably from drought, or killed himself by continually drinking water.

One cold damp day in the beginning of May, I was out in the country on a foraging expedition ; birds' nests and objects of natural history in general being the objects of search. Entering, in the course of exploration, a likely coppice, I descried a blackbird's nest perched among some tangled stems of underwood three or four feet from the ground. A glance at the interior, however, soon showed that some other marauder had forestalled me, as the sole occupants of the nest were some crushed and empty eggshells, and scanty remains of the fluid contents spilt about. 'A weasel,' thought I, but wrongfully, as it happened, for on turning away in dudgeon, a rustling movement among the herbage on the ground a couple of yards off, attracted my eyes and ears; and there I saw the undoubted spoiler of the nest, a large Viper, moving away briskly with his tail in the direction of the nest.

A little knowledge is a dangerous thing, and my slight natural history reading, assisted by bad engravings, had helped me to fancy that I knew the Viper from the common Snake well enough; and so, deciding that this was only a common harmless Snake, I made a plunge at the creature and apprehended him with my unprotected hand. Receiving no bite, I was now confirmed in my idea of the beast's innocence (except in the bird's-nest matter), and decided on adopting him as a pet. So presently set off home, a distance of more than two miles, taking my serpentine friend in my hand. Not always in my hand, however, for to beguile the homeward journey I proceeded to try sundry experiments on the supple backbone and easy temper of the animal, occasionally tying him round my neck and so wearing him for a considerable distance; then twining him round my wrist into a fancy bracelet, and weaving him into various knots and devices according to taste, all this with perfect impunity on my part, and the utmost apparent good humour on his.

On the road, a kind farmer of my acquaintance, whose natural history lore was more practical than my own, endeavoured to convince me that I was 'harbouring a Viper in my bosom', but I was not going to hear my good-tempered playmate called bad names, put my finger into the Adder's very mouth to prove he had no idea of biting, and so passed on, in much conceit with myself as an accomplished herpetologist.

We thus reached home in perfect safety and amity. My brothers and sisters greeted the stranger with some little instinctive horror at first, but got over that feeling when they heard of his innocent nature and amusing capabilities, in proof of which I repeated the necktie experiment etc. About this stage, however, I must mention that he exhibited a somewhat unpleasant phenomenon common to the Snake tribe in general, who can relieve themselves of the torpor consequent on a heavy meal, by disgorging the same when irritated and requiring restoration of their usual activity. The rejectamenta in this case consisted of portions of unhatched young birds, thus confirming the nest robbery.

Being thus lightened, and perhaps stimulated by the warmth of a fire in the room, he was now lively enough, unhappily for me, for on essaying to continue my experiments, by tying him into a double knot, his endurance was at an end; one dart at my finger and a sharp puncture told me that the thing was done. Then, too late, I recollected that the 'Adder is distinguished by a zigzag chain of dark markings down the back', and sure enough the vile creature before me had those very marks. In a rage, I battered his life out with a stick, lest he should do more damage, and then settled down to watch the progress of the poison within my system.

It was not slow to take effect; first the wound looked and felt like a nettle sting, then like a wasp sting, and in the course of a few minutes the whole joint was swollen, with much pain. At this juncture my father, a medical man, arrived from a country journey, and set the approved antidotes to work, ammonia, oil, and lunar caustic, to the wound, having previously made incisions about the punctured spot, and with paternal affection attempted to draw out the poison by suction; but nothing availed, and all sorts of horrid symptoms set in, fainting, sickness, delirium, and fever; the hand and whole arm to the shoulder greatly swollen and discoloured, with most intense pain. This state of things lasted for several days. I forget the exact time, but I was not fully restored for more than a fortnight after the bite.

Since that day I have taken care to put my acquaintance with Serpents on such a footing as to be able at a glance to tell the species of any of our three English Snakes; a piece of useful knowledge most easily gained, and well worth the acquirement.

W. H. Hudson

The snake does not, as Pliny taught us, move by means of its fiery spirit. And we know that snakes, with practically no horizon at all and so short-sighted that they can have no landmarks, do yet possess the sense of direction in a remarkable degree. Thus, there are authentic cases on record of tame snakes travelling long distances back to the home from which they had been removed – incidents similar to those we are accustomed to hear every day with regard to our domestic animals and pets. Apart from such cases, we see from observation of their habits that the snake could not do very well without such a sense. Thus, take the snakes that inhabit great grass countries like the prairies, or, better still, the absolutely flat pampas, where the snake, moving on its belly, is down in the grass and seldom has its head above it. In that temperate climate they do not aestivate but spend the eight or nine warm months distributed over the land. The snake may go a long distance in search of the female ; going to her, he has the wind and the message it conveys to him for guide, but there is no extraneous force, no 'nimble emanations' to lead him back to his accustomed haunts — the home where he passes his long summers and his whole life. At the approach of winter, in May, he returns to his hybernaculum, which he shares with many others of his kind, coming in from all directions and various distances. The wintering site is as a rule in a mound on the plain formed by rodents, armadillos and other excavating mammals, and in one of the old cavities they mass themselves together to drowse away the two or three cold months. It is plain that without a sense of direction the serpent, crawling on his belly through the grass over a flat featureless ground, could not find his way back to the same spot each year.

From *A Hind in Richmond Park*

One hot day in December I had been standing perfectly still for a few minutes among the dry weeds when a slight rustling sound came from near my feet, and glancing down I saw the head and neck of a large black serpent moving slowly past me. In a moment or two the flat head was lost to sight among the close-growing weeds, but the long body continued moving slowly by – so slowly that it hardly appeared to move, and as the creature must have been not less than six feet long, and probably more, it took a very long time, while I stood thrilled with terror, not daring to make the slightest movement, gazing down upon it. Although so long it was not a thick snake, and as it moved on over the white ground it had the appearance of a coal-black current flowing past me – a current not of water or other liquid but of some such element as quicksilver moving on in a rope-like stream. At last it vanished, and turning I fled from the ground, thinking that never again would I venture into or near that frightfully dangerous spot in spite of its fascination.

From *Far Away And Long Ago*

. . . I paid no attention to a sensation like a pressure or a dull pain on the instep of my right foot. Then the feeling of pressure increased and was very curious and was as if I had a heavy object like a crowbar lying across my foot, and at length I looked down at my feet, and to my amazement and horror spied the great black snake slowly drawing his long coil across my instep!

I dared not move, but gazed down fascinated with the sight of that glistening black cylindrical body drawn so slowly over my foot. He had come out of the moat, which was riddled at the sides with rat-holes, and had most probably been there hunting for rats when my wandering footsteps disturbed him and sent him home to his den; and making straight for it, as his way was, he came to my foot, and instead of going round drew himself over it. After the first spasm of terror I knew I was perfectly safe, and that he would not turn upon me so long as I remained quiescent, and would presently be gone from sight. And what was my last sight of him; in vain I watched and waited for him to appear on my subsequent days: but that last encounter had left in me a sense of a mysterious being, dangerous on occasion as when attacked or insulted, and able in some cases to inflict death with a sudden blow, but harmless and even friendly or beneficent towards those who regarded it with kindly and reverent feelings in place of hatred. It is in part the feeling of the Hindu with regard to the cobra which inhabits his house and may one day accidentally cause his death, but is not to be persecuted.

From *Far Away And Long Ago*

From long observation of them I am convinced that small snakes of very sluggish habits do not see distinctly farther than from one to three yards. But the sluggish snake is the champion faster in the animal world, and can afford to lie quiescent until the wind of chance blows something eatable in its way; hence it does not require to see an object distinctly until almost within striking distance.

From *Idle Days in Patagonia*

So I pondered, when my musings under that pine tree were interrupted by the arrival on the scene of a young snake. I cannot say with any degree of truthfulness which of us two was more surprised at the encounter. I picked him up, as I always do when they give me a chance, and began to make myself agreeable to him. He had those pretty juvenile markings which disappear with maturity. Snakes of this kind, when they become full-sized, are nearly always of a uniform shade, generally black. And when they are very, very old, they begin to *grow ears* [author's italics] and seek out solitary places. What is the origin of this belief? I have come across it all over the country. If you wish to go to any remote or inaccessible spot, be sure some peasant will say: 'Ah! There you find the serpent with ears.'

These snakes are not easy to catch with the hand, living as they do among stones and brushwood, and gliding off rapidly once their suspicions are aroused. This one, I should say, was bent on some youthful voyage of discovery or amorous exploit; he walked into the trap from inexperience. As a rule, your best chance for securing them is when they bask on the top of some bush or hedge in relative unconcern, knowing they are hard to detect in such places. They climb into these aerial situations after the lizards, which go there after the insects, which go there after the flowers, which go there after the sunshine, struggling upwards through the thick undergrowth. You must have a quick eye and ready hand to grasp them by the tail ere they have time to lash themselves round some stem where, once anchored, they will allow themselves to be pulled in pieces rather than yield to your efforts. If you fail to seize them, they trickle earthward through the tangle like a thread of running water.

He belonged to that common Italian kind which has no English name – Germans call them *Zornnatter* in allusion to their choleric disposition. Most of them are quite ready to snap at the least provocation; maybe they find it pays, as it does with other folks, to assume the offensive and be first in the field, demanding your place in the sun with an air of wrathful determination. Some of the big fellows can draw blood with their teeth. Yet the jawbones are weak and one can force them asunder without much difficulty; whereas the bite of a full-grown emerald lizard, for instance, will provide quite a novel sensation. The mouth closes on you like a steel trap, tightly compressing the flesh and often refusing to relax its hold. In such cases, try a puff of tobacco. It works! Two puffs will daze them; a fragment of a cigar, laid in the mouth, stretches them out dead. And this is the beast which, they say, will gulp down prussic acid as if it were treacle.

But snakes vary in temperature as we do, and some of these *Zamensis* serpents are as gentle and amiable as their cousin the Aesculap snake. My friend of this afternoon could not be induced to bite. Perhaps he was naturally mild, perhaps drowsy from his winter sleep or ignorant of the ways of the world; perhaps he had not yet shed his milk teeth. I am disposed to think that he forgot about biting because I made a favourable impression on him from the first. He crawled up my arm. It was pleasantly warm, but a little too dark; soon he emerged again and glanced around, relieved to discover that the world was still in its old place. He was not clever at learning tricks. I tried to make him stand on his head, but he refused to stiffen out. Snakes have not much sense of humour.

Lizards are far more companionable. During two consecutive summers I had a close friendship with a wall-lizard who spent in my society certain of his leisure moments — which were not many, for he always had an astonishing number of things on hand.

He was a full-grown male, bejewelled with blue spots. A fierce fighter was Alfonso (such was his name), and conspicuous for a most impressive manner of stamping his front foot when impatient. Concerning his other virtues I know little, for I learnt no details of his private life save what I saw with my own eyes, and they were not always worthy of imitation. He was a polygamist, or worse; obsessed, moreover, by a deplorable habit of biting off the tails of his own or other people's children. He went even further. For sometimes, without a word of warning, he would pounce upon some innocent youngster and carry him in his powerful jaws far away, over the wall, right out of my sight. What happened yonder I cannot guess. It was probably a little old-fashioned cannibalism.

Though my meals in those days were all out of doors, his attendance at dinner-time was rather uncertain; I suspect he retired early in order to spend the night, like other polygamists, in prayer and fasting. At the hours of breakfast and luncheon – he knew them as well as I did – he was generally free, and then quite monopolised my company, climbing up my leg on to the table, eating out of my hand, sipping sugar-water out of his own private bowl, and, in fact, doing everything I suggested. I did not suggest impossibilities. A friendship should never be strained to breaking-point. Had I cared to risk such a calamity, I might have taught him to play skittles.

For the rest, it is not very amusing to be either a lizard or a snake in Italy. Lizards are caught in nooses and then tied by one leg and made to run on the remaining three; or secured by a cord round the neck and swung about in the air—mighty good sport, this; or deprived of their tails and given to the baby or cat to play with; or dragged along at the end of a string, like a reluctant pig that is led to market. There are quite a number of ways of making lizards feel at home.

With snakes the procedure is simple. They are killed; treated to that self-same system to which they used to treat us in our arboreal days when the glassy eye of the serpent, gleaming through the branches, will have caused our fur to stand on end with horror. No beast provokes human hatred like that old coiling serpent. Long and cruel must have been his reign for the memory to have lingered– how many years? Let us say, in order to be on the safe side, a million.

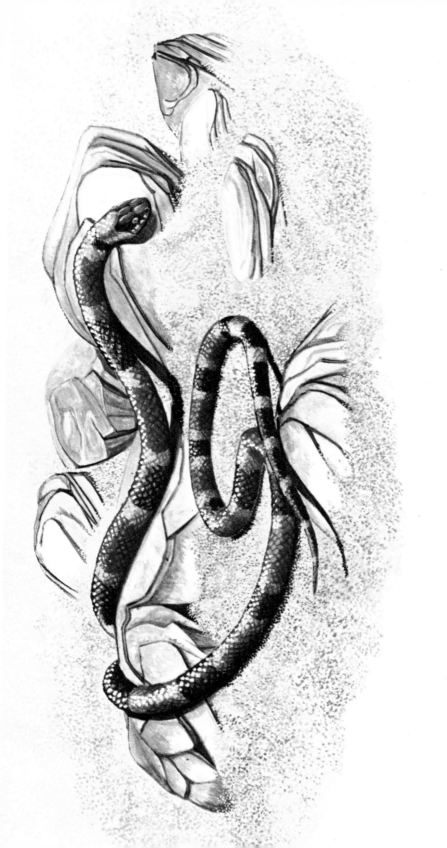

Eastern coral snake (*Micrurus fulvius*). The commonest of the North American coral snakes, found in Florida, Carolina and Texas. Though often gentle when handled, these little snakes are exceedingly venomous.

Journal des Goncourt

27 MARCH 1862

Mi-carême. Dinner with Madame Desgranges. Gautier and his daughters were there . . . the daughters have a peculiar charm, a sort of Oriental languor. They look at you with slow, deep glances from under their splendid thick eyelashes; when they walk they move their arms in a lazy rhythm which they get from their father though they give it an additional touch of feminine grace and elegance. Their charm is not totally French though it is blended with all kinds of French qualities: with almost boyish high spirits, with a way of talking that you would expect from young men rather than girls, with little pouts and grimaces and shoulder-shrugs, tiny ironies displayed in the expressive gestures of childhood. All this makes them very different to well brought-up young ladies; it makes them exquisite little individual creatures whose likes and dislikes are candidly, almost transparently clear . . . One of them, in between flouting her mother who tried to stop her drinking champagne, told me in a low voice about her first convent infatuation, her first love. She was in love with a lizard who used to look at her with its gentle, friend-of-man eye. This lizard was always on her and about her person; it would frequently peep out from her bodice, gaze up at her and disappear again. The poor lizard was crushed by a wicked, jealous schoolfriend and came dragging its entrails behind it to die at her feet. She told me naively that she dug a grave for it and put a cross over it, and that after that she refused to pray and never again went to Mass; that, in fact, from then on religion died in her so revolted was she by the injustice of this death.

Amor y Mambas
Ramón Hernandez

Lengua lengua lengua,
Mi lengua es culebra
Para explorar
El cuerpo divino
De mi Anna adorada.
Culebra culebra culebra,
Anna es una mamba,
Verde y azul.
En los ramos mas altos
Entre el cielo y tierra
Consumamos nuestro amor,
Para siempre, para siempre
Con delicia y terror.

Love and Mambas

Tongue tongue tongue,
My tongue is a snake,
With which to explore
The divine body
Of my adored Anna.
Snake snake snake,
My Anna is a Mamba,
Green and blue.
In the highest branches
Between heaven and earth,
We will consummate our love
For ever, for ever,
With joy and terror.

Alan Moorhead

Here is a short account of how Alan Moorhead, who grew up in a part of Australia where highly venomous snakes such as the tiger snake (see p. 00) were all too common, gradually managed to overcome his fear:

I never saw a snake – that furtive sliminess, that mad, hating eye – without a sudden instinctive constriction of the heart and after the first moment of panic was over we children had just one thought in our minds: 'Kill it. Do not let it get away.' And so we would grab a stick and in a spasm of furious terror we would beat at the hideous twisting thing until at last it lay inert in the dust.

Even then we would not dare to touch it: we would hook it up with the stick and toss it away out of sight into the long grass where ants were bound to demolish it within a day or two . . .

Moorhead goes on to describe his and his contemporaries' superstitious fears which even extended to harmless snakes and some lizards. In 1966 he revisited Australia and spent some time with Eric Worrell, a self-taught herpetologist who was then running a snake-farm at Gosford, 'a stocky, bearded man with very strong arms', who milked snakes (and presumably still does so) for their venom to make antivenene serum. Moorhead visited his farm because he was making a television film about Australian wild-life. Worrell's confidence communicated itself to Moorhead and he was able to go with him into the 'snake-pit', though he could not bring himself to hold a three-foot tiger snake, which Worrell held out to him by the tail. However, he soon began to appreciate the beauty of snakes:

It was a diamond python, six or seven feet long, and I found that after the experiences of the previous day I could look on it, not as an object of horror, but as a living creature; even more than that, as an object of great beauty. There were marvellous markings on its greenish-yellow head, and its diamond-patterned coils flowed round the rafter like some flowering tropical creeper that had grown up out of the ground.

After this Moorhead prided himself that the myth of dread was shattered, but . . .

One does not recover from ingrained irrational fears quite so easily as this. Not three months after I had left Worrell I came across a little adder one day when I was walking along a dry watercourse and instantly habit reasserted itself: I grabbed a stick and beat it to death.

I was sorry afterwards and excused myself on the grounds that it might have bitten someone who had inadvertently stepped upon it in the grass; but then I am not absolutely sure that I would not do the same thing again.

From **Men and Snakes**
Ramona and Desmond Morris

For all its association with evil, death and punishment of wickedness, the Biblical serpent is nevertheless also connected with godly knowledge, healing and immortality. It has been argued that the Egyptian contingent of the Jews in the Exodus may have been snake cultists and Moses himself a kind of snake shaman. He and his partner Aaron were familiar with the famous magicians' trick of the rod and serpent which consists of holding a snake benumbed and stiffened like a stick. Pharaoh called upon his own magicians to take up the challenge. They threw down their rods which also changed into serpents, but were swallowed up by Aaron's snake.

More striking still is the incident of the brazen serpent. After the Exodus from Egypt, the Hebrews, discouraged by the hardships of their journey in the wilderness, murmured against God and against Moses. As a punishment, God sent swarms of fiery serpents against them. Moses, filled with compassion for his people, prayed to the Lord, who instructed him to set up a fiery serpent on a pole so that those who had been bitten, on beholding this image would be cured. It seems rather unlikely that a jealous God would have tolerated the setting up of any image other than his own. The prophets too complained bitterly about the tenacity with which the Jews clung to snake worship and the Nehustan or brazen serpent, with its miraculous healing properties, was worshipped for more than five centuries. Eventually the idol was broken and completely destroyed by the reforming King Hezekiah and the old serpent became the adversary of the new God.

Weston La Barre had put forward the intriguing and original theory that the ancient Near Eastern rite of circumcision (which, as practised by the Jews, dates back to the Old Stone Age) was originally connected with the cult of the snake. He argues that 'The snake obtains immortality by sloughing off its skin. Ergo, as the snake is immortal through sacrificing and leaving off a part of himself, so man may also be saved by ritually sacrificing a part of himself. If snake = phallus, then snakeskin = foreskin. . . . Snake: immortal: sheds skin: :phallus: immortality: circumcision.'

The snake continued to be worshipped by the Ophites, a Gnostic body whose ideas flourished in the first six centuries of Christianity. Because of their attempt to reconcile Christianity with the teachings of various Greek and Oriental philosophers, they were treated as heretics by the Church. The sect of the Nassenes, for example, claimed that the serpent who tempted the first couple was not the Devil, but the incarnation of Christ. The Prohibition against eating the fruit came from a jealous god who wished to keep men in a state of slavish submission to his will. Having been persuaded to eat the fruit by the serpent, man became aware of his divine origin and was transformed from a state of unconscious limitation to one of conscious freedom. Consequently they taught that knowledge rather than mere faith was the key to salvation.

The Nassenes worshipped Christ as the serpent and celebrated a curious ceremony, the Eucharist of the Serpent, which they termed the perfect sacrifice. St Epiphanius, Bishop of Constantia, in his treatise *Panakeion*, describes this ritual as follows: 'They pile up loaves of bread upon a table, they summon the serpent they keep as a sacral animal. The basket is opened, he comes out, goes to the table, writhes among the loaves and transforms them into the Eucharist. Then they break the bread among which the serpent has moved about and distribute it to the communicants. Each one kisses the serpent on his mouth, for the animal has been tamed by incantation, and prostrate themselves before the sacred animal. Thus the Supper consists in making the Logos present in the serpent's body. The serpent, by contact, consecrates the loaves. He gives, once the holy elements have been absorbed, the kiss of peace, and carries to God the thanksgivings of the faithful.'

On Gnostic gems and amulets, which were greatly valued for their magical powers, the Supreme Being is sometimes portrayed as a serpent with seven or twelve rays about its head. Other talismans show Abraxas, the source of the 365 emanations, a strange composite figure. He has the body of a man, the head of a cock or hawk and twin serpents as legs. In one hand he carries a scourge, in the other, a shield. He was addressed as 'Thou who presidest over the mysteries of the Father and the Son, who shinest in the night time, holding the second rank, the first Lord of Death'.

The Gnostics of the Manichean system believed that Christ dwelt in the sun and returned there when his time on earth was completed. They claimed that the Great Serpent that glided over the cradle of the Virgin Mary when she was aged one and a half years and Christ was therefore the incarnation of the Great Serpent. Although the Ophites as a group were doomed to fade from the scene, Gnosticism lingered on into the Middle Ages and had a considerable influence on Christianity.

Even in the New Testament a striking parallel is drawn between the snake, the ancient symbol of resurrection and immortality, and Christ: 'And as Moses lifted up the serpent in the wilderness, even so must the Son of man be lifted up; that whosoever believeth in Him should not perish, but have eternal life.'

The Story of a Snake Story

In 1930 James Stern wrote a short story, 'The Man Who Was Loved', which was first printed in *The London Mercury*, has since been reprinted several times and appears in *The Stories of James Stern*. The background was Rhodesia, which Stern knew well. The chief character was a Major Carter, a Scot by birth, a congenial, convivial, knockabout person who dealt in horses, cattle and dogs and enjoyed conducting distinguished visitors from the station to the Grand Hotel of the town. (Stern had Bulawayo in mind.)

Major Carter had spent several years of his life in Australia where there are probably more highly poisonous snakes than anywhere else in the world and he had developed his own method for dealing with them. 'He would creep up behind them, grab them by the tail-end, then swing them round and round till he cracked their heads off in the air, as a huntsman cracks a riding crop. It may sound improbable, but this and the fact that he had pleasing manners with mothers and their manless daughters, could tell good stories and drink much whisky with men, account for his having earned the love and admiration of the people of every colour in the town.' Stern, who tells the story in the first person, then describes how he was motoring across the veldt with the Major and they came on a large black mamba in the middle of the road. There were four natives with a team of terrified oxen. The Major jumped out of his car. ' "Come on!" he cried. "Here's some fun!" ' . . . he took his coat off, rolled up his sleeves and rubbed his hands, 'his eyes fixed in glee to the hateful object on the ground. . . .

'The Major . . . bent himself almost double: stretching his left leg straight out behind him, he moved towards his poisonous prey by pressing the foot of his stiff leg into the ground to steady himself, while his right foot in some extraordinary manner stole silently forward, inch by inch. His right arm he held out but a yard from the snake, whose entire attention was still occupied watching the frightened oxen, and his open shirt hung so loose from his shoulders that I could see his chest and the red hairs growing down to his navel.

'Suddenly, with a bound and a cry like that of an animal as it leaps upon another in fury, the Major had snatched the snake from the earth and was whirling it round and round his head at such a speed that it was unable to coil itself, and the sound it made whistling through the air was like that of wind whining through the rigging of a ship. As the snake's head drooped on its wild circuit through space and ceased to make further effort to coil, the Major seemed to lift the whole weight of his body onto his right foot as suddenly he changed the course of his whirling, and, as a huntsman wields a long-lashed riding-crop, cracked the length of the reptile above his head in the air. As he did this he uttered a low whoop of triumph and let go the tail-end of the snake. I watched it soar into the sky, and then, though obviously headless, saw it coil itself and fall yards away into the depths of the bush.

'I had just taken a deep breath of relief and was about to clap my hands with joy at the Major's fantastic performance, when I heard a howl, and looking up, saw him clutch his stomach as he dropped like a falling tree to the ground.

'With the natives I rushed to his side, and in a strangled voice heard him cry: "A knife! Quick! For God's sake! It's got me! It's . . . *got* me!" And with the last word his hand fell away from his stomach, his head rolled back upon the ground. . . .

'In one quick and feverish movement the Major's own native tore away the shirt from his master's body. And at the same moment, uttering a sharp scream, he jumped back. We all jumped away from what we saw. For lying on the Major's bare stomach was the bleeding, fangless, though not yet motionless head of the mamba!'

The rest of the story describes the Major's funeral and there is a subtly conveyed but definite intimation that four young Africans who carry the coffin are the Major's sons. . . .

So much for the story. In 1952 Stern was living near Sherborne on the border of Dorset and Somerset. A lady who kept a bookshop in Sherborne told him there was a blind man who lived close by who very much wanted to meet him. They met and the man said: 'I cannot understand it. That story of yours, "The Man Who Was Loved", describes my uncle to the life. And that was exactly how he died. But how could you have known because he died years after you wrote the story.'

Selected Bibliography

BARBOUR, T. *Reptiles and Amphibians, Their Habits and Adaptations*, Houghton Mifflin Co., New York, 1934.

BELL, T. *A History of British Reptiles*, Van Voorst, London, 1849.

BELLAIRS, ANGUS, *The Life of Reptiles*, 2 vols., Weidenfeld & Nicolson Ltd, London, 1970; Universe Books Inc., New York.

BELLAIRS, ANGUS. *Reptiles*, Hutchinson University Library, London, 1968; Harper & Row Inc., New York, 1960.

BOULENGER, G. A. *The Snakes of Europe*, Methuen & Co. Ltd, London, 1913.

CARR, A. *The Turtle, A Natural History*, Cassell & Co. Ltd, London, 1969.

COLBERT, E. H. *Dinosaurs*, Hutchinson & Co. Ltd, London, 1962; E. P. Dutton & Co. Inc., New York, 1961.

DITMARS, R. L. *Reptiles of the World*, Macmillan & Co. Ltd, London, 1966; The Macmillan Co., New York.

FAYRER, J. *The Thanatophidia of India*, Churchill, London, 1872.

KLAUBER, L. M. *Rattlesnakes*, 2 vols., University of California, 1956.

MORRIS, RAMONA and DESMOND. *Men and Snakes*, Hutchinson & Co. Ltd, London, 1965; MacGraw-Hill Inc., New York.

PARKER, H. W. *Snakes*, Robert Hale & Co., London, 1963; W. W. Norton & Co. Inc., New York.

POPE, H. H. *The Reptile's World*, Routledge and Kegan Paul Ltd, London; Alfred A. Knopf Inc., New York, 1955.

ROLLINAT, R. *La Vie des Reptiles de la France Centrale*, Libraire Delagrave, Paris, 1934.

SCHMIDT, K. P. and INGER, R. F. *Living Reptiles of the World*, Hamish Hamilton Ltd, London, 1957; Doubleday & Co. Inc., New York.

SMITH, MALCOLM. *The British Amphibians and Reptiles*, William Collins Sons & Co. Ltd, London, 1951; British Book Centre USA, New York.

Index

132-141